꧁꧁꧁꧁ CHICHESTER TOWERS ꧂꧂꧂꧂

The Duke of Newcastle. By Isaac Gosset. From the collection of the late
Admiral The Honorable Sir Herbert and Lady Meade-Fetherstonhaugh,
of Uppark.

CHICHESTER TOWERS

BY L. P. CURTIS

YALE UNIVERSITY PRESS

NEW HAVEN AND LONDON, 1966

For
ASHLEY OLMSTED
and
FRANCIS STEER

HISTORICAL COMEDY is never written. Authors of historical novels have merely to imagine the past as the readers like to see it. Writers of serious biography have critically to examine records of fact as handed down by the actors or their contemporaries, and then, without smile or grin, adopt what Meredith describes as an ironical habit of mind—"to believe that the wishes of men . . . are expressed in their utterances". Historical farce is largely based on the cheap device of conscious anachronisms, and therefore does not count. But historical comedy would require the most accurate and most detailed knowledge and understanding of men and circumstances; for it would have to ascertain and recognise the deeper irrelevancies and incoherence of human actions, which are not so much directed by reason, as invested by it *ex post facto* with the appearances of logic and rationality. It is more difficult to grasp and fix the irrational and irrelevant than to construe and uphold a reasonable but wrong explanation, and this is the greatest difficulty both in dealing with contemporaries and in writing history.

SIR LEWIS NAMIER, *England in the Age of the American Revolution*

CONTENTS

THE GIST of the story unfolded in *Chichester Towers* is simple: a certain archdeacon happened to be offered a deanery in an English cathedral and wrote a letter containing reasons why he should decline the offer. Ordinarily one would ignore the incident because something was tried and ended in failure. Such a matter, we may suppose, is not history: history consists in things that get done. But unfortunately for people who like to take shortcuts in history and quite fortunately for people who like to pause and enjoy the humor that is in history, the archdeacon's letter is a masterpiece in its way, a masterpiece of eighteenth-century servility and cunning, and only with difficulty can one dismiss it from the memory. In his letter the archdeacon shows himself to be a character who might have come straight out of an eighteenth-century stage comedy, so sharp yet so sinuous are the strokes with which he draws his own portrait. He makes us want to know more about him. We find ourselves at least startled to discover that an archdeacon should appraise the filling of an Anglican deanery in such exclusively political terms. Questions rise up about the archdeacon and his world and even about history itself, and the questions have a way of staying for answers. Why was he considered worthy of the deanery? Why could he not quite bring himself to shut the door on so tempting an offer of preferment? What circumstances of power enabled a local politician, albeit a duke and courtier enjoying employments under the Crown, to make the offer? With what even greater politician had this duke conferred about the appointment? How far were the archdeacon's self-denying motives inspired by his own self-interest and the environment of Church, State, and local society in which he moved and had his being? To what extent does the episode of his equivocal refusal open a way into the heart of an entire civilization? And may we conclude that his altruism is as significant a clue to the character of the civilization in which he flourished so merrily as were the great legislative debates of the time, the deeds of heroes, and the compositions of genius?

Once answers to such questions begin to shape themselves, the incident, which had at first seemed simplicity itself, develops, as is the way of most sequences, into inconceivable complexity. The archdeacon's friends and relations also have their own friends and relations. All sorts of forgotten people, politicians no less than clergymen, peers, a galaxy of bishops and deans, rectors, vicars, canons and prebendaries, shopkeepers and farmers, come crowding onto the stage, one man leading to another, until the question of the proffered deanery is almost lost in convolutions composed of dozens of self-seekers whirling round and round in what all of us know, if we stop to reflect, is in truth the dance of life.

At first glance the lives they lived seem utterly different from our own. In their parochial security they took sides on what must appear to be trifling issues. Most of them fawned upon the great landowners of the county and thought little of traveling forty or fifty miles to pay their respects to their patrons. They liked nothing better than to obtain a post for a friend: doing so heightened their standing in the community. In their letters the politicians, as might be expected, wrote letters about politics. The clergy in their letters also wrote about politics. Indeed the clergy wrote about politics to the virtual exclusion of religion, although on ecclesiastical matters they were sticklers for law and precedent. In conduct and in expressed opinions the people in this tale appear to have been of an age only. Their motives, of course, are timeless.

The story made by their mutual relationships is not one of drums and trumpets. It is in no way ennobling or even important in the sense that national history is important. The story of the deanery of Chichester is local history. The greatness of

xii

English civilization in the eighteenth century, if by greatness we mean Pope or Blackstone or Chatham or Johnson or Nelson, will not show in the men and women here described or mentioned—except for one puissant duke, who must surely have been the hardest-working duke in history. Let it suffice that the story holds the mirror up to England in the eighteenth century: on its ecclesiastical side the story could be roughly duplicated in more than half the counties of England; and on its political side it reflects the rough-and-tumble of electioneering in every English county. Patently and notwithstanding its absurdities, the story uncovers the foundations of a great civilization, in that the society disclosed is free, well ordered, confident, buzzing with vivacity, and just stupid enough to be politically wise. That its imagination is captivated by the urgency of trivialities (once we forget about the hopes, the needs, and the frequent disappointments of the people concerned) is, of course, a matter for comedy.

Every format has its decorum. I cannot hope to thank in print all those who have helped me in the writing of this essay. I am chiefly indebted to the following owners or guardians of manuscripts: the Trustees of the British Museum; Lady Zouche, Mr. P. A. Tritten, and the Honorable Clive and Mrs. Pearson; the Duke of Richmond and Gordon; Lord Sackville and Mr. F. M. Mason; Sir Robert and Lady Gooch; the Dean and Chapter of Chichester; the Henry E. Huntington Library. Unpublished Crown Copyright material in the Public Record Office is reproduced by permission of the Controller of Her Majesty's Stationery Office.

To the generosity of the late Admiral The Honorable Sir Herbert Meade-Fetherstonhaugh, G.C.V.O., C.B., D.S.O., I owe permission to reproduce the wax portraits of the Duke of Newcastle and Henry Pelham. The Dean and Chapter of Chichester have allowed me to reproduce their portrait of the Reverend Thomas Ball.

For encouragement and giving me of their special knowledge I am indebted in particular to Miss W. D. Coates, Dr. Nelly Kerling, Mrs. Wallace Notestein, Mrs. Donald Hyde, the late Sir Lewis Namier, and Messrs. Romney Sedgwick, Aubrey Newman, J. H. Plumb, John Harrison, Ashley Olmsted, John McDill, Hector Kinloch, Lewis Wiggin, W. G. Hiscock, Wilmarth Lewis, George Lam, Herman Liebert, C. Beecher Hogan, Robert Metzdorf, W. H. Dunham, Jr., A. S. Foord, F. W. Hilles, John Blum, and David Horne. Among my friends in Sussex I owe special thanks to K. W. Dickins, W. D. Peckham, C. E. Welch, A. A. Dibben, and, above all, the Archivist of West Sussex, Francis Steer.

NOTE

Since the second Duke of Richmond plays a major role in this essay, the reader may well ask why the Goodwood Papers contain so little material relating to the situation described. Not even important documents printed by the Earl of March in *Records of the Old Charlton Hunt* and in *A Duke and His Friends* were found among the papers. With the generous aid of His Grace's secretary, Miss Pamela Taylor, Mr. Steer and I made a thorough, if vain, search of Goodwood House and its outbuildings; since then, the Duke himself has pursued the quest, but without success. Fortunately, sufficient material has survived in other sources to persuade me that in essential outlines the story of the deanery of Chichester is about complete.

L. P. C.

New Haven, Connecticut
December 1965

xiv

THE PRINCIPAL PLAYERS

THE POLITICIANS

The Duke of Newcastle — one of His Majesty's Principal Secretaries of State

The Duke of Richmond — Brigadier General and Master of the Horse

The Duke of Dorset — Lord Warden of the Cinque Ports

The Duke of Somerset — an elder statesman living in retirement

Henry Pelham — brother of the Duke of Newcastle and Member for the County of Sussex

James Butler — Member for the County of Sussex

The Earl of Middlesex — eldest son of the Duke of Dorset and candidate for the County of Sussex

Thomas Sergison — an Opposition candidate for the County of Sussex

Sir John Miller, Bt. — a self-important squire

Sir Cecil Bisshopp, Bt. — a leader of the Opposition in Sussex

John Page — an independent Member for Chichester

THE CLERGY

Edmund Gibson — Bishop of London

Thomas Bowers
Edward Waddington
Francis Hare
Matthias Mawson
} successively Bishops of Chichester

Thomas Sherlock John Newey Thomas Hayley James Hargraves William Ashburnham	successively Deans of Chichester
Walter Barttelot	a clerical beggar and Prebendary of Chichester
Thomas Gooch	brother-in-law of Thomas Sherlock and Canon Residentiary of Chichester
William Sherwin	Canon Residentiary of Chichester
John Parke	a troublemaker and Canon Residentiary of Chichester
John Backshell	Canon Residentiary of Chichester and brother-in-law of Thomas Gooch
Thomas Ball	an accomplished wire-puller and both Archdeacon and Canon Residentiary of Chichester
William Clarke	a laughing scholar and Canon Residentiary of Chichester
Robert Austen	a poor curate

ONE. THE SETTING

THE GAME was something like musical chairs, or rather, it was a looking-glass version of musical chairs: for while the number of chairs remained constant, if a player dropped out, all the other players scrambled to get better, more commodious seats, and new adventurers came in to play too. The game was played to a lively tune (a theme and infinite variations), and the name of the tune was 'Influence'. None knew when the game had begun or imagined that it would ever end. The game was part of the nature of things. Played across the length and breadth of eighteenth-century England, it constituted the core of local politics and reached to men's hearths and their dearest ambitions. Peers played it, and so did the gentry, lawyers, merchants, army and naval officers, freemen and freeholders, artisans, shopkeepers, and their dependents. Clerics seemed to play the game throughout their professional lives. Some of the players won, some lost; others could never discover how or where to break into the gay circle. The game resulted directly from the alliance of Church and State. It was therefore a political game. The ancient partnership of Church and State secured advantages to each: the State got the influence of religion in support of Government and was on the whole freed from clerical hostility; the Church, in return for an Erastian surrender of independence, received a public endowment for the clergy, a significant voice in the House of Lords, coercive authority for its courts, and, finally, the earthly comforts of the Test Acts.[1] The game, like the alliance, went down to the roots of English society. Nowhere was it played with more avidity and skill than in Sussex, home of the Pelhams and the diocese of Chichester.

1. William Warburton, *The Alliance between Church and State* (London, 1748), Pt. II, chap. iii, and Pt. III.

Sussex in the early eighteenth century was a wilderness with many human figures. Except for the Downs, which stretched along its coastline like smooth-backed whales, Sussex was heavily wooded. It was, in fact, the most wooded county of England. Timber made shipbuilding the principal industry of the ports and provided the charcoal for the local iron industry, from which the Ashburnhams and the Fullers drew much of their wealth. Here and there one came across chalk, lime, and cement works. The chief occupation was farming, and the Southdowns of Sussex were destined to make not a little stir in the world.[2]

Even though the county has rightly been called a backwater,[3] Sussex people liked to travel, and went stumbling and jolting along the miry roads. 'Foreign' travelers like Celia Fiennes and Defoe lamented the blind, dark lanes and the mud: near the town of Lewes, Defoe saw 'an ancient lady, and a lady of very good quality . . . drawn to church in her coach with six oxen . . . the way being so stiff and deep, that no horses could go in it'.[4] The roads were in truth symbols of inadequate prosperity and parochial shiftlessness. The wonderful new agriculture of the later eighteenth century did not begin here. By 1741 the iron industry was rapidly decaying for want of a substitute for charcoal. Rivers and harbors of towns were silting up. Smuggling throve—sometimes with violence. Most of the inhabitants of the county perforce contented themselves with farming enclosed fields or keeping shop or practicing crafts in villages and towns.

In contrast to five southwestern counties, Cornwall, Devonshire, Somerset, Dorset, and Wiltshire, where the political influence of the gentry dominated throughout the eighteenth century, the soil of Sussex lay under ducal influence. There

2. *Victoria History of the County of Sussex, 2* (London, 1907), 169 ff.

3. G. H. Nadel, 'The Sussex Election of 1741', *Sussex Archaeological Collections, 91* (1953), 91. Hereafter cited as *S.A.C.*

4. Daniel Defoe, *A Tour through England and Wales* (Everyman's Library), *1,* 129.

large estates belonged to no less than five dukes—Newcastle, Dorset, Somerset, Norfolk, and Richmond. Among numerous important seats were Newcastle's Halland and Dorset's Stoneland Lodge in the eastern division, and Somerset's Petworth House, Norfolk's Arundel Castle, and Richmond's Goodwood House in the West. Among the gentry were the Ashburnhams of Broomham, the Gages of Firle, the Bisshopps of Parham, the Hays of Glyndebourne, the Peachcys of West Dean, and the Barttelots of Stopham.

Each of the two divisions of Sussex had a county town: Lewes in the east and Chichester in the west. Neither place had a population of as much as 4,000. The city of Chichester was handsome. The spire of the early Norman cathedral soared upward above the ridges of ancient red-tiled roofs. The two main streets intersected at right angles in the blunt fashion of the Romans who had laid them out, and at the intersection rose the ornate, early sixteenth-century City Cross. The city had formerly been noted for its malt works. Certain merchants of the town milled wheat and shipped it by boat to London. Others imported Portuguese wines. Among these was Henry Peckham, familiarly known as 'Lisbon', who lived at Pallant House, one of the handsomest brick mansions of Chichester. Defoe was not impressed by Chichester: it had neither the stirring commerce of Wisbech nor the gaiety of Bury. 'I cannot say much for the city of Chichester,' he observed, 'in which, if six or seven good families were removed, there would not be much conversation, except what is to be found among the canons, and dignitaries of the cathedral.'[5]

Here in Sussex in the autumn of 1741 a fresh round of the game of musical chairs took place. The Dean of Chichester was said to be dying, a successor must be provided, and the county was undergoing a contested by-election.

Inherently the death of a dean and his replacement are not remarkable enough to justify detailed exposition. The thing

5. *A Tour through England and Wales, 1*, 134.

is common. What makes the death in 1741 of the Dean of Chichester of much more than passing interest is not the abundance of surviving sources about the episode nor yet the brilliant spotlight they throw on several of the many personalities concerned. The Dean's death and the events that led up to and followed it reveal a society in political action.

The autumn of 1741 was for the English a time of crisis, but among the people of Sussex the crisis went almost unnoticed. Britain was at war with Spain on behalf of Captain Jenkins' ear and her own trade, and the war by 1741 not only was being fought ineptly but was merging into a greater conflict, the War of the Austrian Succession. The general election in May of that year had further reduced Sir Robert Walpole's Whig majority in the House of Commons by losing him some twelve seats.[6] His fall from office was expected. Sussex was undergoing a by-election. The Dean was dying. So one thing impinged upon another from Walpole's Houghton in Norfolk to the deanery at Chichester and made the choice of a new dean an event that reveals in absorbing subtley the connections, the influence, and the assumptions of men within the pyramidal structure of eighteenth-century society. The story belongs to the times in so far as it shows the ingrained principles of social subordination and nepotism at work as well as the dominion of landed proprietors. Each member of society in Sussex had needs and ambitions; most had something to sell; and all relied on his or her connection with someone more influential than himself to do him favors. Time had necessarily organized these needs and ambitions into a recognizable pattern. Collectively they served to thrust men into Parliament no less than to govern both the county of Sussex and the diocese of Chichester.

Yet there is also something almost too familiar about the story, for these men played the game of politics in a society where no one group, however successful, could ever hope to suppress its rivals. Players in politics are obliged to make mutual accommodations. They must therefore pull wires. In

6. John B. Owen, *The Rise of the Pelhams* (London, Methuen, 1957), pp. 6–7.

4

eighteenth-century Sussex they pulled a prodigious number of wires. They were not unlike the politicians of any twentieth-century democracy: similar provincial interests and the doing of favors for relatives and friends; the greatest people, rarely in position to use force and unable to buy an entire electorate, pull even more wires than do the lesser folk in order to persuade them to do their bidding. Thus eighteenth-century society is disclosed in the half-round, on its political side, and the elaborate reticulations of connection in Sussex served as an example in miniature of the political nation itself. The alliance between Church and State is seen in action. It supplied underpinnings of political power at Westminster. How the underpinnings were guarded and made profitable to the politicians, no less than the role of the Church in such actions, requires the stitching of a picture in petit point. The little things that happened to certain people at Chichester late in 1741 reached in their meanings back to the past and forward into the future.

But first let us look at the groups into which the people of Sussex were divided. There were several; they represented different interests; and a few of them were involved in both the choice of a dean at Chichester and the parliamentary contest over a member for Sussex. Of least account but sufficiently strong to excite alarm were the Roman Catholics, of whom the Duke of Norfolk at Arundel was the passive leader. The Nonconformists, particularly numerous at Lewes, were more to be wooed than dreaded. The political Opposition in the county scarcely harbored Jacobite yearnings. It may have been Tory and was sometimes described as such; it was certainly anti-Walpole, anti-excise, and anti-Newcastle. To the Duke of Newcastle and his friends the Opposition was the 'enemy', sometimes 'the Country Party'. It was led by country gentlemen (some of whom were relatives), notably by Sir Cecil Bisshopp of Parham, John Fuller of Brightling, and Thomas Sergison of Cuckfield, all of whom had been unsuccessful candidates in the Sussex elections of 1734. The Duke of Newcastle, head of the house of Pelham, together with his allies and agents, formed the principal political interest and supported the Whig administration of Sir Robert Walpole. In the western half of the county the Duke of Newcastle worked with the Duke of Richmond, with 'Tanky' (the Earl of Tankerville of Uppark), uneasily with James Lumley of Stansted; in the east Newcastle could count on the assistance of the Ashburn-hams and their connections, and on the Duke of Dorset. Dorset headed his own parliamentary bloc, which consisted of his three sons, his uncle the Earl of Wilmington of Compton Place, Eastbourne, the egregious Bubb Dodington, and his three members in the House of Commons. If, at Westminster, Dorset and his friends were currently enemies of Sir Robert Walpole and flirting with the parliamentary Opposition,[7] in Sussex Dorset was willing enough to work with Newcastle, who in spite of rumors to the contrary did remain faithful to Walpole. The aged Duke of Somerset and his allies, the Peacheys of West Dean near Chichester, formed a tertium quid, Somerset wobbling between esteem for the Pelhams and adherence to principles that inclined him to support Opposi-tion. At Chichester lived a fairly independent group—Sir John Miller, 'Lisbon' Peckham, Hutchins Williams, John Page, and their friends. At Chichester too were found the cathedral folk and their considerable political influence. All over the county the loyalty of the parish clergy to the Whig cause needed watching and encouragement.

The first intimation to reach the Duke of Newcastle of the likely demise of the Dean of Chichester came from the Rev. Walter Barttelot. On October 1 from Rottingdean on the Sussex coast Mr. Barttelot informed Newcastle that Dean Hargraves was 'in a very dangerous and declining way'[8] and asked to succeed him in the deanery.[9]

7. Owen, *The Rise of the Pelhams*, pp. 13, 14 n., and passim.
8. Cf. the Rev. Roger Thwackum to Mr. Allworthy: 'If the vicar of Aldergrove should die (as we hear he is in a declining way), I hope you will think of me . . .' *Tom Jones* (1749), Bk. XVIII, chap. iv.
9. Barttelot to Newcastle, Rottingdean, 1 Oct. 1741. British Museum,

Walter Barttelot was an invalid and a clerical beggar. Not satisfied with the rectory of Rottingdean and, over the Downs, the vicarage of Selmeston, as well as a prebend in Chichester Cathedral to which he had been preferred twenty years before, he had long fancied that there was nothing on earth he so much desired as to be a canon residentiary of Chichester and thereby a member of the influential Chapter. His chance came in 1737 when a residentiaryship fell vacant. Barttelot asked Newcastle for the favor, although the right of election to the Chapter ostensibly belonged to the dean and canons residentiary, and he assured the Duke that he would employ no small part of his residence 'in cultivating and improving such an interest for your Grace's friends both in the church and country round it, as may at least equal that of any other clergyman whatever'. The Duke put him off, being already engaged to promote another prebendary of Chichester to the first vacancy among the residentiaries.[10] Again, two years later, although 'both gouty, infirm, and of an age superior to any' of the four residentiaries (he was then fifty), he pinned his hopes on living to see 'another vacancy among the residentiaries' and, knowing well the Duke's habit of ensuring a Whig future by means of present promises, ventured to intimate his continuing ambition to be himself a resident. As proof of his steadfastness to 'that particular interest at the head of which your Grace has for many years past so eminently distinguished your self', he told Newcastle that he had kept with him for a whole week the rector of St. Peter and Blessed Mary Westout, Lewes, in an effort to persuade him to return to the Duke's interest.[11]

Newcastle Papers, Add. MSS, 32698, fols. 92–93. Hereafter all references to the Newcastle Papers are by catalogue mark only.

10. Barttelot to Newcastle, Rottingdean, 4 April 1737: 32690, fols. 268–69. Newcastle to Barttelot, Newcastle House, 7 April 1737: 32690, fol. 270.

11. Barttelot to Newcastle, Rottingdean, 3 Sept. 1739: 32692, fols. 266–67.

Barttelot had, it must be admitted, persuasive power. He was heir to his father's Elizabethan mansion and the manor of Stopham near Pulborough. Barttelots, like Pelhams, counted themselves among the oldest families in the county and had been lords of the manor of Stopham since the fourteenth century. For many generations they had pursued the even tenor of their ways, possessing good lands and unambitious dispositions, content with obscurity and the highest esteem of their neighbors. As a potential squarson, Walter could wield his own and his father's interest: he could direct certain freeholders how to vote. He took pride in his influence. Such he had emphasized to Newcastle in 1737, and now again in 1741 he assured him that in respect to interest he considered himself 'inferior to none of my brethren, nay I will venture to promise your Grace at this ensuing as well as any future county election as many votes as can be reasonably expected from any person of my profession throughout the diocese'.[12] There were some twenty freeholders in the parishes of Stopham, Fittleworth, and Coates,[13] besides a possible handful at Selmeston. 'Not one of my little flock at Rottingdean will go astray,' he told Newcastle with velvet delicacy. They were not likely to wander into the fold of the Duke's opponents in the approaching election: not only was Barttelot planning an entertainment for them and offering to give some twenty-five freeholders bed and board at Rottingdean, should the election be held at Lewes, but Lord Middlesex, Newcastle's candidate in the present contest for the county and eldest son of the Duke of Dorset, patron of Rottingdean, had promised to send some venison against the festivities.[14] Useful as he could prove himself to be, Barttelot must have appeared to New-

12. Barttelot to Newcastle, Rottingdean, 1 Oct. 1741: 32698, fol. 92.

13. James Dallaway, *The Parochial Topography of the Rape of Arundel in the Western Division of the County of Sussex* (London, 1832), 2, Pt. i, 286, 346, 351.

14. Rev. Thomas Hurdis to Newcastle, Seaford, 13 Sept. 1741: 32698, fol. 41.

castle too insignificant, too unpracticed in the arts of politics and government to be dean of Chichester. The prospect might be laughable. The likely death of Dr. Hargraves was quite another matter.

As things went at Chichester, James Hargraves was both illustrious and invaluable. He lacked, to be sure, Barttelot's roots in the soil of Sussex. He appears to have owned no landed estate in the county; he could not talk of influencing his humble tenants; he was strictly a professional. Yet in his climb up the ladder of preferment from Wakefield in Yorkshire, where he was born in 1690, he had, partly by his talents, partly by his zest, picked up mighty patrons along with good preferments in their gift. Storie Exhibitioner from Wakefield Grammar School,[15] he had completed his formal education at Clare Hall, Cambridge, where, taking his degree in 1711/12, he had known the Duke of Newcastle, who probably took up residence at Clare in 1710.[16] Henceforth the bright world opened to him. He was a Fellow of the college for ten years. Newcastle, one may assume, got him the rectory of East Hoathly, in which parish lay Halland, his Grace's principal residence in Sussex. Hargraves published a couple of sermons. He married a daughter of an archdeacon of Lewes,[17] became a prebendary of Chichester and chaplain in ordinary to the King. George II by royal mandate added to his academic embellishments by making him a doctor of divinity in 1728. Next year the Duke of Dorset presented him to one of his Sussex livings, the rectory of Waldron near Uckfield.[18] In

15. Matthew Henry Peacock, *History of the Free Grammar School at Wakefield* (Wakefield, 1892), p. 189.

16. It is unlikely that Hargraves, as John Nichols states (*Literary Anecdotes,* 9 vols. London, 1812–15, *1,* 416 n.), was Newcastle's tutor at Clare. Cf. Stebleton H. Nulle, *Thomas Pelham-Holles, Duke of Newcastle. His Early Political Career, 1693–1724* (Philadelphia, 1931), p. 10.

17. James Dallaway, *A History of the Western Division of the County of Sussex* (London, 1815), *1,* Pt. i, 139.

18. *S.A.C., 13* (1861), 86.

1730, as the new rector of St. Margaret's Westminster (he had been a prebendary of the collegiate church since 1725), he baptized Lord March, infant heir to that power in western Sussex, the Duke of Richmond.[19] Thus enriched by the countenance of three dukes, all of whom possessed estates and influence in Sussex, Dr. Hargraves had not failed to show his gratitude by exerting himself in the great electoral contest for the county in 1734. He had wooed voters with joints of venison from Halland. He had approved a landowner's 'good dispositions' in declaring that, should any of her tenants at Ticehurst vote for the Opposition candidate, she would turn them all out of their farms.[20] He inched his way further into Newcastle's esteem and conscience by taking young Master Pelham, the Duke's cousin, into his house for instruction.[21] His due reward came in 1739: upon the death of Dean Hayley he was promoted at Newcastle's recommendation to the deanery of Chichester.

The Chapter of Chichester was an oligarchy of five. Formerly the Chapter had been a great chapter and consisted of the dean, precentor, chancellor, treasurer, the archdeacons of Chichester and Lewes, and thirty-one prebendaries. But finding that the revenues of the cathedral church, when divided among the multitude of residentiaries, no longer sufficed to maintain the old, laudable hospitality which became their station, Bishop Curteys by an ordinance of 1574 reduced the Chapter to five: four canons residentiary and the dean.[22] There resulted the administrative Chapter, a close corporation, election to which was nominally by cooptation. The

19. *Sussex Notes and Queries, 10* (1945), 110.

20. Basil Williams, 'The Duke of Newcastle and the Election of 1734', *English Historical Review, 12* (1897), 470. Hargraves to Newcastle, E[ast] Hoadly, 19 Aug. [1733], 32688, fol. 148.

21. Hargraves to Thomas Pelham of Stanmer, 5 Nov. 1737: 33085, fol. 529.

22. F. G. Bennett, R. H. Codrington, C. Deedes, eds., *Statutes and Constitutions of the Cathedral Church of Chichester* (Chichester, 1904), p. 26.

duties of this inner Chapter varied. The Dean and Chapter looked after the rentals and fines of their considerable estates, the receipts from which in 1741 amounted to £641.[23] Besides regulating the cathedral services, they appointed all the cathedral servants from the sometimes unruly vicars choral down to the sextons. They named the master of the grammar school and the prebendary of Bargham. Out of 286 livings within the diocese the Dean and Chapter, together with the bishop, were the patrons of some 46, 33 of them lying in the archdeaconry of Chichester in western Sussex.[24] In addition, the Dean and Chapter held the exceptionally rich vicarage of Amport in Hampshire and during these years always assigned it to one of their body.

Such circumstantial evidence of political influence wielded by the Dean and Chapter was not all. Exclusive of Chichester, they owned in Sussex upward of 68 properties, at least 50 of them lying in the western division of the county.[25] At Chichester itself, a town of 785 houses in 1740,[26] they got income from no fewer than 92 properties. Edmund Gibson, who had been Precentor of Chichester since 1703 and taken pains to reside there, knew well, in 1717, their political importance:

23. West Sussex County Record Office, Cap. I/5/2, 'A Rental of the Dean and Chapter of Chichester, 1720–68'. Canon Gooch in 1735 estimated the annual income of the Dean and Chapter to be about £1,500 a year, including the vicarage of Amport, worth about £400. Gooch to Newcastle, Chichester, 31 Oct. 1735. Public Record Office, State Papers Domestic [hereafter cited as P.R.O., S.P.], 36/36 fol. 150.

24. Figures based on John Lloyd, *Thesaurus Ecclesiasticus* (London, 1788), pp. 84–95; Alexander Hay, *The History of Chichester* (Chichester, 1804), pp. 608–33; George Hennessy, *Chichester Diocese Clergy Lists* (London, 1900); Nadel, 'The Sussex Election of 1741', p. 97; Thomas Ball's 'Liveings in the Gift of the Dean and Chapter of Chichester' [3 Dec. 1736]. P.R.O., S.P. 36/39 fol. 111 (enclosure).

25. 'A Rental of the Dean and Chapter'.

26. West Sussex County Record Office, Lists and Indexes, No. I, 'List of the Number of Persons within the City of Chichester', 31 Dec. 1740, fol. i.

'the balance on the Whig side, which is in that city depends a great deal, if not wholly, on the Dean and Chapter, and their influences in all elections.'[27] So tempting a morsel as the Dean and Chapter did not escape the Whig managers a decade later. By 1741 the Dean and Chapter had become a sort of pocket borough of the Duke of Newcastle and his ally, the Duke of Richmond.

For the past twenty years the appointment of sound Whig diocesans had been easy enough. Bishop Bowers (1722–24) was an old friend of the Pelhams, an adviser to both Newcastle and his father (Bowers owed his elevation to the see of Chichester to the Duke);[28] that learned and farsighted statesman, Edmund Gibson, Bishop of London and Sir Robert Walpole's ecclesiastical minister from 1723 to 1736, picked the next Bishop of Chichester, Edward Waddington (1724–31);[29] Waddington's successor, Francis Hare (1731–40), had been Walpole's tutor at King's and Marlborough's chaplain and was Newcastle's candid friend; Bishop Matthias Mawson (1740–54) toed the Whig line.

But to capture the Dean and Chapter of Chichester for the Duke's pocket was quite another matter: it required patience and watchful alertness. They were five instead of one and of much greater political might in the city. A 'false step' in electing a new residentiary, Gibson had warned back in 1717, and Whig interests at Chichester could 'never . . . be retrieved'; transfer capitular strength to 'the Tories' and it would be 'in vain to set up any Whig for member of Parliament there'.[30]

Off and on for a century after 1688 the Chapter was in

27. Gibson to Wake, Westminster, 14 Sept. 1717: Wake MSS, 20, Christ Church, Oxford.

28. Newcastle to Bowers, Claremont, 6 June 1723: 32686, fol. 258. Francis Hare to Newcastle, 12 May 1737: 23690, fol. 285.

29. Norman Sykes, *Edmund Gibson, Bishop of London, 1669–1748* (London, Oxford University Press, 1926), p. 84.

30. Gibson to Wake, Westminster, 14 Sept. 1717. Wake MSS, 20.

turmoil, and the turmoil sprang from the near side of politics. In 1688 the Chapter had staged a chilling, vain revolt against James II's nominee for dean.[31] When in 1727 Gibson's bishop, Edward Waddington, held his primary visitation of the cathedral, he found the Dean and Chapter aligned against him.

Little political breezes dusked and shivered through Chichester Cathedral in that year. Little disputes took on the character of seismic convulsions that the contenders affected to still. In 1727 the formidable Thomas Sherlock had been dean since 1715. Master of the Temple and Hoadly's principal adversary in the controversy over Convocation, he was destined to become one of the most eminent divines during the reign of George II. He was always jealous of the rights and privileges of the Church and he had the scholarship, eloquence, and tenacity to defend them. Taken 'reeking hot out of the midst of the Tories (of which body he is still most assuredly a member)', Gibson caustically remarked, Sherlock was 'to be cast immediately into a nest of Whigs' at Chichester.[32] Sherlock was suspected of Jacobitism and of wishing to rally the Tory clergy around him. At Chichester he appears to have worked fast. His brother-in-law, Dr. Thomas Gooch, a strong Tory and Master of Caius College, Cambridge, was elected into the Chapter in 1719 and joined forces with Canon William Sherwin (elected 1717/18) and Sherlock's devoted henchman, John Parke (elected 1723). Except for Thomas Hayley (elected 1712), the son of a former dean of Chichester, the Chapter in 1727 contained at least three Tories, was anti-Gibson, and was prepared to resist the demands of Gibson's Whig bishop, Edward Waddington, and his ambitious, resourceful ally, the Rev. Thomas Ball. In short order, upon Waddington's visitation, Chichester Close was by the ears, and the anger resembled

31. W. D. Peckham, 'Chichester Non-Jurors', *Sussex Notes and Queries,* 9 (1944), 115–16.

32. Gibson to William Nicolson, 5 Nov. 1715. Quoted in Norman Sykes, *William Wake, Archbishop of Canterbury, 1657–1737* (Cambridge, Cambridge University Press, 1957), 2, 101.

that which Archdeacon Grantly and his adherents felt upon the arrival of Barchester's new bishop, Dr. Proudie, and his chaplain, the Rev. Mr. Slope.

At his primary visitation of the cathedral in May 1727 Bishop Waddington challenged the jurisdiction of the Dean and Chapter in several ways. He insisted upon visiting St. Mary's Hospital at Chichester. The Hospital was an ancient charitable foundation, similar to Hiram's Hospital at Barchester. St. Mary's housed and sustained five aged and infirm persons. It was in the patronage of the Dean and Chapter, and in 1727 Dean Sherlock was Warden of the Hospital. Waddington also desired to appoint an usher to the Chapter's school and, worse still, he insisted upon naming as well as paying his own verger to conduct him from the palace to divine service in the cathedral without so much as the Chapter's leave.

At the same time, the young Rev. Thomas Ball was making an infernal and exasperating fuss. He charged Sherwin, the President of the Chapter in the absence of Hayley, with acting illegally when he executed the Bishop's mandate to admit him to the prebend of Hampstead. Ball appealed to Waddington for justice. He joined other Whig schismatics among the prebendaries, notably Gibson's protégé and Waddington's chaplain, Isaac Maddox, and 'Johan' Hargrave:[33] together they defied the Chapter in its choice of a proctor at Convocation and elected their own. Messages passed hastily between the Bishop's palace and Sherlock's deanery. Capitular records were ransacked in order to translate claims into rights. Sherlock, who was learning to hate Ball, hinted to Waddington that Ball did nothing but by the Bishop's direction and asserted that Ball had actually applied to Canon Parke to install him instead of to Parke's superior, Sherwin, in order to pro-

33. Almost certainly an error. The future Dean of Chichester, James Hargraves, was Prebendary of Thorney. He had preached and published the sermon at Waddington's consecration in 1724.

voke jealousies within the Chapter. Tempers flared and reached a climax one day at evensong. That morning Waddington had tried how far he might proceed with respect to his verger: he had gone to the cathedral accompanied by one of his own servants wearing a proper gown and carrying a long black staff crowned with a silver miter. Waddington may have expected opposition: he met with none from the Dean and canons residentiary, and at the end of the service he gave the blessing, as usual, and returned to the palace in the same manner as he went, undisturbed. At evensong, when the Bishop again attended the service, matters went differently. Canon Gooch, who had read prayers in the morning, read them again in the afternoon and had now determined to ignore Waddington's presence. As the Bishop was about to rise up to give the blessing, he saw Gooch's eye upon him, and 'his tongue was too quick for me for he concluded the service himself with the Grace of our Lord Jesus Xit'.[34]

Ferrets for precedents, the lions of the cathedral did on this occasion try also to be lambs. But shortly after they had reached agreement, Sherlock in 1728 resigned the deanery to become at the Queen's behest Bishop of Bangor and Gibson's open rival at Court. Henceforth Sherlock cooperated with Government, although detesting Gibson, and associated with Newcastle on terms of considerable intimacy. As the body moved, so did the shadow. Gooch, whose sole merit, it was said ungenerously, was to be brother-in-law to Sherlock,[35] likewise came to heel. He promised Newcastle his support in the contested election for Sussex in 1734. Maneuvered by Sherlock into a succession of bishoprics, Gooch, upon being translated to Norwich in 1738, vacated his residentiaryship. In 1735

34. West Sussex County Record Office: Ep. I/49; Cap. I/7/1, fol. 65 ff.; Chapter Act Book, *3*, fol. 78 ff.

35. John Percival, Earl of Egmont, *Diary, 1730–1747* (Historical Manuscripts Commission, 1920–23), 2, 250. John Venn gives a judicious account of Gooch in his *Biographical History of Gonville and Caius College, 3* (Cambridge, 1901), 115–24.

Canon Sherwin had died. Thus between 1728 and 1738, in consequence of the resignations of Sherlock and Gooch and Sherwin's death, three vacancies opened in the Chapter of Chichester.

Newcastle filled at least two of them and approved the presbyter, who succeeded Sherlock in the deanery. The new dean was John Newey, a mild man and a brother-in-law of Bishop Waddington's. In 1734 Newcastle showed his regard for Dean Newey by granting his request and procuring a fellowship at Merton for Newey's son.[36] The next year Sherwin's death precipitated an unusual crisis within the Chapter, and Bishop Hare's extraordinary, almost whimsical solution.

In the choice of a successor to Sherwin the surviving members of the Chapter—Newey, Hayley, Gooch, and Parke—had reached by May 1735 a deadlock issuing directly from the intricacies of connection and politics. Newey, who was now much indisposed, and Hayley, ever attentive to Newcastle's interest, wanted Thomas Ball. Gooch and Parke (so John Dear, a future mayor of Chichester, told the Duke) were carrying things 'very high' on behalf of their own candidate, the Rev. John Backshell. 'If not prevented', Dear went on to say, Ball's appointment would establish Newcastle's interest in the church of Chichester, since Ball would prove himself a loyal second to Dean Newey and an ally of Canon Hayley's as against Canons Gooch and Parke. Dear pointed out that the cathedral clergy enjoyed 'a very considerable influence on many freeholders both in the city and the country, who are either their tenants or dependents'. These, he added, would be of great consequence to Newcastle.[37]

'If not prevented.' Dear was well aware of a threat to Newcastle's ascendancy not only within but outside the Chapter. In Dear's opinion, John Backshell, rector of Burton *cum* Coates, near Petworth, and a prebendary of Chichester since

36. R. Meadowcourt to Newcastle, Merton College, 4 Aug. 1734: 32689, fol. 341.

37. John Dear to Newcastle, Chichester, 11 May 1735: 32690, fol. 34.

Sherlock's day, was something of a political menace on account of his near relations. Until Canon Sherwin's death had opened to him the prospects of becoming a residentiary, Backshell had 'ever acted in the opposition', as indeed one may surmise from his having stood surety for Gooch back in 1727 upon the latter's second marriage. In 1727, presumably with that opponent of Chichester Whiggery, Canon John Parke, officiating, Gooch married a daughter of Sir John Miller of West Lavant, near Chichester.[38] Backshell, having already married her sister, thereby became Gooch's brother-in-law.[39] The two marriages brought the sisters' nephew, young Sir John Miller, into the orbit of the Chapter's affairs. Sir John's estate near Chichester may have puffed him up. He was now convinced that he must put pressure on Newcastle if he was to bring his uncle Backshell into the Chapter ahead of Thomas Ball. He tried impertinence. 'Upon the death of Dr. Sherwin,' he wrote to the Duke, 'I was surprised to hear your name made use of in opposition to Mr. Backshell's being a residentiary, who is my near relation, and equally your friend as well as Mr. Ball.'[40] Sir John thought of his own prestige, not of Newcastle's, in wishing to secure his uncle's election into the Chapter ahead of the Duke's man, Ball. Were this favor not granted, Sir John was threatening to revert to his family's principles (his father and grandfather had in turn represented Chichester) and so would in future 'oppose the Court'.[41]

Not, of course, that Miller's influence in and around Chichester was really so considerable as people said: 'his mean and abject way of liveing' had made him so negligible that were

38. The marriage took place in Parke's Subdeanery. Sussex Record Society, Vol. 12: *Sussex Marriage Licenses. Deanery of Chichester, 1582–1730,* comp. Edwin Dunkin (1911), 168.

39. John Comber, *Sussex Genealogies. Horsham Centre* (Cambridge, 1931), pp. 15–18. Sussex Record Society, Vol. 12: *Sussex Marriage Licenses. Deaneries of Pagham and Tarring, 1579–1730* (1911), 246.

40. Miller to Newcastle, Chichester, 9 May 1735: 32690, fol. 30.

41. Dear to Newcastle, Chichester, 11 May 1735: 32690, fol. 34.

he disposed to compliment Newcastle with his interest 'twould be of little use'. Newcastle could secure Miller and Backshell later on.

What now pressed was Ball's promotion. Newcastle must realize that a 'crisis' had come about. Easily may Dear have imagined the state of the Chapter as the result of Backshell's election: it would then consist of two Whigs only, the aged and ailing Dean Newey and sickly Canon Hayley, ranged against those implacable triumvirs, Gooch, Parke, and Backshell. Appalling thought! Matters had indeed reached 'a crisis, when the interest of the Church is to be either secured or lost forever'.[42] Dear, like Edmund Gibson eighteen years before, vaticinated disaster to the Whig cause in Chichester and perhaps in more than Chichester should a false step now be made.

But why a false step just now? The year before, in 1734, in the hot contest for the county of Sussex, Gooch and Backshell had gone together to the polls and voted for Newcastle's two candidates.[43] Surely the brothers-in-law were now loyal to the Duke, although linked to their cocky nephew, Sir John Miller. Why then did Dear insinuate his suspicions of their present loyalty? Did he calculate that Pelhamite alarm, once aroused, must end in gratitude to himself and therefore serve his own advancement?

Ball also had his way of keeping Newcastle from complacency respecting the state of the Chapter or from overlooking his services. To make himself indispensable he too insinuated. Gooch, he wrote some weeks later as he looked back upon the crisis, would never have carried his opposition so far in the matter of Ball's coming into the Chapter singly, had he either been awed by Dean Newey (even as Bishop Waddington had once been awed by Canon Gooch) or not been so nearly related to Backshell. And Ball added significantly: Gooch would never have gone to extremes had he not been

---

42. Dear to Newcastle, Chichester, 11 May 1735.
43. MS Poll Book for the county election [1734]: 33059B, fol. 27^v.

18

'perhaps supported underhand by a superiour'.[44] Ball alluded, of course, to Gooch's brother-in-law Sherlock, now Bishop of Salisbury and bitterest foe of Walpole's ecclesiastical adviser, Edmund Gibson, Bishop of London. In venturing this insinuation Ball may have been trying to disquiet the Duke.

And not without good reason. How Ball knew that Gooch was receiving advice from Bishop Sherlock with regard to the Chapter is not clear, but, then, few secrets seem to have been kept in eighteenth-century Chichester. Possibly Ball even knew that as far back as 1732 Gooch and Sherlock had been laying plans to bring Backshell into the Chapter ahead of Ball. Early in September of that year Gooch wrote to Sherlock a letter (now unfortunately lost) in which he described the struggle for power going on both within and without the Chapter. The letter probably informed Sherlock that Canon Hayley was in poor health and that he desired Ball to succeed him as residentiary. The letter seems also to have expressed Gooch's hopes of eventually succeeding Canon Sherwin in the wardenry of St. Mary's Hospital—a post that Gooch may have desired more for the prestige it would give him in Chichester than for its paltry salary of about £46 a year.[45]

Sherlock, in reply, took up the linked problems of the two rival candidates, Ball and Backshell, and of the wardenry of the Hospital. Remembering Ball's intrigues of 1727, Sherlock warned his brother-in-law that if Ball were to be elected instead of Backshell, then the Chapter would be 'all to pieces soon' and suggested that if Gooch could not succeed in electing Backshell, he and Canon John Parke ought to mount their assault from another angle by proposing William Clarke, who, as the Duke of Newcastle's chaplain, could not possibly fail of election. As to the Hospital, Sherlock declared that were he in Gooch's place he would 'part with the Hospital twice

44. Ball to Newcastle, Chichester, 3 Oct. 1735: P.R.O., S.P. 36/36, fol. 139.

45. C. A. Swainson, 'The Hospital of St. Mary, in Chichester', *S.A.C.*, *24* (1872), 61.

over' in order to bring Backshell into the Chapter.[46] What did Sherlock mean by this advice? Without Gooch's missing letter it is impossible to know for certain. Still, from the terms on which the capitular dispute was settled no less than from the eventual succession of the wardenry a conjecture may be ventured. Sherlock, it seems, was urging a compromise within the struggle for power: if, when a vacancy occurred among the residentiaries, Gooch could manage to carry Backshell's election ahead of Ball's, then Gooch should yield his claim to succeed Sherwin in the Hospital to the other party within the Chapter, namely to Dean Newey, Canon Hayley, and finally to their apparent candidate for the wardenry, Ball, once he had become a residentiary.

Sherwin's death in the spring of 1735 brought about the expected crisis. Gooch now found himself in the awkward situation of having Sherlock at his ear while he himself tried both to bow before Newcastle and advance the cause of his distrusted brother-in-law, John Backshell. Once again Sherlock warned Gooch that to bring Ball into the Chapter at this time would be 'putting every thing into the power of Hayley and Ball' and he saw correctly that the capitular deadlock resulted from Gooch's and Parke's negative upon the Dean and Hayley.[47]

For his part, when he addressed himself to Newcastle, Gooch scoffed at fears. He would make the Duke easy. He had, as he assured Newcastle some months later, entered into 'the service of your Grace, and the ministry, with heartiness of zeal' and was conscious 'of no one deviation'. He supposed that Newcastle knew how he and Backshell had voted in the late election for the county until he was shocked to learn of the Duke of Newcastle's displeasure because he had heard a base and scandalous report that Backshell had declared he

46. Sherlock to Gooch, 11 Sept. 1732: Gooch Papers, Benacre Hall, Wrentham. Microfilms of the Gooch Papers are deposited at the Colonial Williamsburg Research Library.

47. Sherlock to Gooch, Temple, 8 May 1735: Gooch Papers.

'could not in conscience vote for Mr. Pelham and Mr. Butler'.[48]

But in May 1735 Gooch, having shifted his ground, was himself at ease regarding Newcastle's interest. He hoped, he wrote to the Duke, that an accommodation of the dispute could be reached to Newcastle's and the Duke of Richmond's liking; were such an accommodation not to their joint interests, no relation (by which Gooch meant his two brothers-in-law) or consideration whatever should prevent his closing with Ball's friends. The single objection, he told the Duke, to Backshell's admission was that 'Mr. Parke will get strength'. But this notion was so far from being the truth that from that moment Parke would cease to be Gooch's proxy (the trust would pass, and so it did, to brother Backshell), and Parke would 'never more have the power' he had had in the Chapter. Gooch talked at length with both Sir John Miller and Canon Hayley. Eventually he accepted the latter's Gilbertian resolution that the Chapter invite Bishop Hare, in view of Dean Newey's likely death in the near future, to admit both Backshell and Ball to its body and divide the profits of the single place between them.[49] Hare consented. In August he clapped both men into the Chapter with this proviso: Backshell, being some years older than Ball, was to be admitted first; but as a mark of his respect for the Dean, who had espoused Ball's interest, Backshell must waive to Ball all claim by seniority to the wardenry of St. Mary's Hospital whenever that place, into which Gooch had entered on Sherwin's death, should again be void.[50] Ball, now more grateful to Newcastle than ever, yet ventured to express his doubts about the outcome of the 'great affair'. 'We', he wrote, still lacked 'an indisputable

48. Gooch to Newcastle, Chichester, 3 Oct. 1735: P.R.O., S.P. 36/36, fol. 141.

49. Ibid., 9 May 1735: 32690, fol. 32. Hare to Newcastle, London, 14 Oct. 1735: P.R.O., S.P. 36/36, fol. 145.

50. West Sussex County Record Office, 'Chapter Act Book', 3, fols. 115–16.

superiority' in the Chapter. But 'we', that is, Dean Newey, Canon Hayley, and himself, had 'the ballance at least', as against Canons Gooch, Backshell, and Parke.[51]

Five weeks later Dean Newey died, and once again the Chapter was at the center of turmoil. The question facing Newcastle was precisely Churchill's on becoming First Lord of the Admiralty in 1911: do you promote on the basis of meritorious seniority or do you accept Admiral Lord Fisher's taunt that 'Favouritism is the secret of efficiency'? In the event, Churchill promoted Beatty 'over the heads of all to this incomparable command', the Battle-Cruiser Squadron. Not being Churchill, Newcastle wobbled between regard for loyal seniority and belief that younger talent would best support the King's government. His dilemma confirms his charity and fairness as well as his sense of strategy. How could Church and State best be served? By Dr. Thomas Hayley, the senior residentiary, who for years had been inviolably attached to the true interest of the government and was now at the age of fifty-four 'old, and infirm'? Or by Dr. Hargraves, rector of East Hoathly and one of His Majesty's chaplains, whose zeal for the King's service was, Newcastle wrote, 'equal to any body's and his abilities are inferior to few . . . I can answer for his unshaken fidelity to the King's person and government, and for his character in every respect'. Newcastle laid the matter of who should be Dean of Chichester at His Majesty's feet, hoped that the offer would first be made to Hayley ('it would be a great comfort and satisfaction to him') and hinted that since his taking the deanery 'might weaken the interest of the government in the Chapter . . . means may be found out, possibly, to induce him to decline' the deanery, so that Hargraves could be preferred.[52]

To resolve his dilemma Newcastle needed not only royal

51. Ball to Newcastle, Chichester, 8 Aug. 1735: P.R.O., S.P. 36/35, fol. 125.

52. Newcastle to Harrington, Whitehall, 16 Sept. 1735: P.R.O., S.P. 43/88.

assent but diplomacy at Chichester. For his part, the King approved the recommendation of Hargraves, agreed that the deanery be offered first to Hayley, and ordered a warrant to be made ready for the royal signature, the moment he heard of Hayley's refusal.[53] As for the diplomat on the spot, Thomas Ball must call upon Hayley and in fairness sound him out.

Ball so did, being, as he wrote, much obliged for the 'particular confidence reposed in me upon this occasion'. He called. In the strongest terms he advanced arguments why in his private opinion Hayley's acceptance of the likely offer would be neither for his own nor for the public interest. The arguments seemed to stagger Canon Hayley. But upon reading Newcastle's own letter, the ambitious canon 'grew very eager and resolute in an instant' and to Ball's astonishment bombarded him with reasons why he must accept the deanery— the gracious offer from Their Majesties by Newcastle's means was too generous to be resisted; the expected fine, left by the late Dean, would do more than defray the extraordinary costs; as for capitular politics, why, Gooch and Backshell were beginning to be ashamed of their old ally, Canon Parke, and would now be the more ready to join 'us', since they would be pleased by the appointment; moreover, Hayley had no doubts that, should they desert, he could so divide them as to gain his point, for indeed it was never known in the church of Chichester that a dean of spirit and experience, especially when supported by 'a sure second', could fail of having 'a superiour influence and authority in the Chapter'; and finally, Hayley was certain that Gooch would never have carried his opposition so far in the late fracas had he been awed by Dean Newey. If Hayley intended to be a spirited dean, Ball, his sure second, was not so confident about the outcome. He ended his letter by admitting to the Duke that his "poor services" were not always as successful as they were sincere and went on to assure him that he would never 'fail to execute your com-

53. Harrington to Newcastle, Hanover, 4 Oct. 1735: P.R.O., S.P. 43/88.

mands with the utmost exactness . . . tho' I shou'd not always be able or lucky enough to prevail'.[54] On the same day Hayley sent Newcastle his acceptance and thanks.[55] A pretty kettle of fish.

Within a week Hayley's ambition provoked a fresh and preposterous crisis. He let it be known at Chichester that he intended to take the almost unprecedented step of keeping his residentiaryship along with the deanery. Gooch warned Bishop Hare of Hayley's intention. Hare scolded and in turn warned Newcastle. Hayley, citing a precedent of 1660, temporized but was obliged to yield to the combined threats of both the Duke and the Bishop.[56] He became Dean in the following January, and the Chapter returned to the customary number of five.

If back in 1735 Newcastle had momentarily lost control of the Chapter, plans, well laid by the assiduous Ball, prevented a further crisis upon the next vacancy. As early as January 1735/6 Ball had advised the Duke that he might depend upon the loyalty of Gooch and Backshell so long at least as the former had 'such high and promising expectations' of becoming a bishop.[57] Gooch was himself now stepping forward to claim a reward for his recent services to Newcastle at Chichester. In veiled language that formed a measure of good manners when one asked a favor of the Duke of Newcastle, Gooch in February expressed his wish for such perferment 'as may make it agreable to me to part with my present station at Chichester'.[58] He was made Bishop of Bristol in 1737 and

54. Ball to Newcastle, Chichester, 3 Oct. 1735: P.R.O., S.P. 36/36, fol. 139.

55. Ibid., fol. 140.

56. For the controversy over Hayley, see ibid., fols. 143, 145–47, 149–53; 36/38, fols. 1, 7, 10–11, 15, 20, 26.

57. Ball to Newcastle, Chichester, 4 Jan. 1735/6: P.R.O., S.P. 36/38, fol. 7.

58. Gooch to Newcastle, Chichester, 1 Feb. 1735 [/6]: P.R.O., S.P., 36/38, fol. 26.

upon being speedily translated to Norwich resigned his residentiaryship in 1738.

Ever since the autumn of 1735 Ball, it seems, had been trying to arrange matters so that Newcastle's chaplain, that unpolitical fellow, 'honest' William Clarke, might at the next vacancy reinforce the Duke's true friends within the Chapter. Ball had supposed that Gooch and Backshell would also support Clarke's candidacy—as 'a proper proof of their sincerity' —provided that Sherlock, Bishop of Salisbury, had no other prebendary to recommend to them.[59] Ball's surmise was correct. Sherlock welcomed the acceptance of his alternative proposal of 1735 and allowed Gooch to obtain Backshell's promise to support Clarke. So upon Gooch's resignation in 1738, thanks in good measure to Ball's diplomacy, Clarke succeeded Gooch in the Chapter without protest from anyone, and Ball succeeded Gooch at the Hospital. Finally, when in 1739 Dean Hayley died, the Duke listened to Bishop Hare's suggestion to 'take your measure about a successor'.[60]

Dr. Hargraves was at length appointed.

Thus by 1740 the Chapter was seemingly over its difficulties and dutifully Whig except for the doubtful Backshell and that leftover of the bad old days, Canon Parke.

Now amongst the cathedral set at Chichester John Parke was notorious—a thorn in Church-Whig flesh. His life showed how a poor Lancashire boy could rise through the university and the Church to bequeath at his death considerable property near Chichester and in Hampshire.[61] In 1741 he was about fifty-three years old. Fellow of St. John's at the time of Sherlock's vice-chancellorship of the University of Cambridge, he may have come into the diocese of Chichester as the result of Sherlock's encouragement and patronage. Here he picked up

59. Ball to Newcastle, Chichester, 3 Oct. 1735: P.R.O., S.P. 36/36, fol. 139.

60. Hare to Newcastle, Chichester, 8 Aug. 1739: 32692, fol. 212.

61. Prerogative Court of Canterbury (cited hereafter as P.C.C.): Penfold 23.

two livings and in 1719/20 was collated to the valueless prebend of Middleton, which at least gave him some prestige and set him in line for possible election into the administrative Chapter. Three years later, with Sherlock still dean, he was chosen a residentiary. On the eve of Sherlock's promotion to the see of Bangor he penned his gratefulness in the Parish Register of Subdeanery. With a shade of truculence he wrote: 'Doctor Thomas Sherlock, our most worthy Dean and who is universally esteem'd the greatest man of his profession in the kingdom . . .'[62]

John Parke had in truth been obnoxious. In the general election of 1734, as Ball complained to Newcastle, Parke and 'Lisbon' Peckham of Chichester were 'indefatigable' agents of Sir Cecil Bisshopp and John Fuller, Opposition candidates for the county of Sussex.[63] Parke proved to be enough of a menace in that exacting contest to oblige Newcastle to write not only to Parke's patron, Sherlock, but also to Gooch in order to beg their admonition to Canon Parke. Readily Newcastle owned to Sherlock 'that the clergy in general are extremely well disposed, many of them most zealous and highly incensed at the Opposition'. He regretted that he could not

> reckon Mr. Parks of Chichester amongst the number. He is very active against us, and it is the more remarkable, as I believe he is the only one of the Church that is. I wish your Lordship would be so good as to write him, in such manner as you think proper. I am persuaded Mr. Parks cannot say, we ever did any thing personally to offend him; and I was in hopes our publick behaviour would have recommended us to his favour.

Thus Newcastle let his essential integrity shine before Bishop Sherlock. 'I write', he continued, 'by this post to Dr. Gooch . . . As Mr. Parks is more upon the spot than any of the other

62. West Sussex County Record Office, Parish Register of Subdeanery, 5, 75.
63. Ball to Newcastle, Chichester, 4 Nov. 1733: 32689, fols. 9–10.

Residentiaries, I am afraid he will influence some who depend upon the Chapter.'[64] Sherlock promptly obliged by enclosing the requested admonition in his reply to Newcastle under a 'flying seal' and had his letter to Parke postmarked at Bangor lest Parke suspect it had not come directly from him. 'If my friend has been active already,' Sherlock wrote, 'I doubt whether I shall succeed . . . I write to him in earnest, tho' tenderly for fear he should start at the apprehension of being influenced.'[65] Gooch also knew Parke for a difficult independent: 'What my brother Parke means, I cannot guess. The Bishops of Chichester and Bangor are the persons, who have the greatest (but, I fear small will be greatest) influence over him.' Parke, he continued, had ventured to approach him about his second vote in the forthcoming Chichester election. Would Gooch give it to the Tory Colonel Yates? Gooch with some humor was inclined to reply that he wished to give no vote to a man who opposed Newcastle's family but would vote for the Colonel on condition that Parke vote with him for Newcastle's candidates for the county.[66]

Parke, as shall appear, was not alone in resisting the spreading influence of the Pelhams and their connection. In May 1734, on the eve of the election for the county, which was to be held in the cathedral city, just as the Bishop of London and the Archbishop of Canterbury were lending their support to the Duke and just as Ball was busily preparing the Bishop of Chichester's palace and stables to accommodate Newcastle and his retinue, seeing that the beds were fitted and aired and the house stocked with conveniences for 'breakfasts and other liquors,' just as Ball was contriving these arrangements in order to convince Hare's dependents that the Bishop was 'in good earnest about the election and put it out of Mr. Parke's power to persuade the people that his lordship is indifferent

64. Newcastle to Sherlock, Hampton Court, 4 Sept. 1733: 32688, fol. 258.
65. Sherlock to Newcastle, Bangor, 8 Sept. 1733: 32688, fol. 297.
66. Gooch to Newcastle, Cambridge, 6 Sept. 1733: 32688, fols. 281–82.

upon this trying occasion,' Parke made a fresh attack upon Newcastle's candidates for the county in the Hundred of Manhood, where he had property and influence over voters.[67] Equally to be deplored, Parke in October 1740 had cooked up a scheme whereby he would get himself chosen residentiary of Salisbury, whither Sherlock had been translated from Bangor. Boastful, he made no secret of his intentions. Dean Hargraves took offense.

> As Mr. Parke [he wrote to Newcastle] is a very troublesome man here, I should not dislike the exchange with the approbation of my superiors, but there being no law that I know of to hinder a man from being residentiary in two churches. If Mr. Parke obtains a stall at Salisbury, with the assistance of the bishop, and retains his here at Chichester, it will certainly enable him to do more mischief than I can wish him power to be able to do.[68]

The venture failed: Parke never became a canon of Salisbury or of any other cathedral church. His fortunes declined with the extension of Newcastle's and Richmond's control of the Chapter. After 1736 he received no additional preferment except that gorgeous prize, the vicarage of Amport, valued the same year at £400 and in 1770 at between £400 and £800 a year,[69] a peculiar of the Dean and Chapter, in fact their 'best living', to which Parke fell heir by right of seniority in the Chapter, notwithstanding James Pelham's fatuous belief that 'the Bishop and the whole countrey are astonished that Parks should carry off the great living of Amport' and that it ought to go to the support of the Dean.[70] Amport, together

67. Ball to Newcastle, Chichester, 6 May 1734: 32689, fol. 228.

68. Hargraves to Newcastle, Chichester, 24 Oct. 1740: 32695, fol. 331.

69. Ball's list of 'Liveings in the Gift of the Dean and Chapter': P.R.O., S.P. 36/39, fol. 111. Jeremiah Markland to William Bowyer, 28 Aug. 1770: Nichols, *Literary Anecdotes, 4,* 351.

70. Col. James Pelham to Newcastle, Broomham, 25 Sept. 1739: 32692, fol. 324.

with Parke's now insignificant prebend of Middleton and his residentiary's place, constituted his preferment for the rest of his life. One wonders what variations on the theme of mischief he yet managed to compose. His little machinations had sufficed: they annoyed, as doubtless he intended them to annoy; at times it must have seemed that Parke might topple the Chapter into the Opposition camp. Backshell's opinion of Parke is unknown; Clarke in his mild way was possibly too amused by the absurdities of local politics to care; but Hargraves and Ball detested Mr. Parke, and Richmond once accused him of Jacobite sympathies.[71] At the worst they could always alert Newcastle, since in their regard the Chapter of Chichester, being of only less moment than one of the parliamentary boroughs of Sussex, must likewise be nursed, wheedled, and coddled along in the Duke of Newcastle's interest.

None can deny to Thomas Pelham-Holles, Duke of Newcastle, a foremost place among the political artists and bosses of history. In English politics no less than in English government he played a significant role for over fifty years. Nowhere was there so busy a man as Newcastle and, unlike Chaucer's Man of Law, he really was busier than he seemed to be. That is a reason why people noticed that he was always in a hurry and why one statesman described him as 'hubble-bubble'. Newcastle had reason to be in a hurry. In 1741, in addition to being Vice-Admiral of Sussex, High Steward of the University of Cambridge, and Lord Lieutenant of the counties of Middlesex and Nottingham, he had been Secretary of State for the Southern Department since 1724. The duties were manifold, and, as if they were not enough to keep him busy, he thought little about 'poaching upon a colleague's preserve'.[72] From his office he supervised, jointly with the Secretary of State for the Northern Department, domestic order

71. Richmond to Newcastle, Goodwood, 1 Dec. 1742: 32699, fol. 549.
72. Mark A. Thomson, *The Secretaries of State, 1681–1782* (Oxford, 1932), p. 101.

and police and recommended persons to fill the county offices; he kept an eye on Ireland and Scotland; besides carrying out his duty to correspond with the governors of British colonies, he had most of the colonial patronage in his hands; he conducted His Majesty's diplomatic relations with the courts of France, Spain, and other southern European states, garnered the recommendation of envoys within his own province, and in 1739 took charge of the war by sea and by land against Spain. In those days a successful statesman had to have support in Parliament. Newcastle had his own followers in the House of Commons. In the Lords, where he served as one of Sir Robert Walpole's lieutenants, he supported Lord Chancellor Hardwicke's defense of Sir Robert's administration against the formidable attacks of Opposition during the fateful years 1740 and 1741. News from a distance came and went by letters and dispatches. Newcastle read thousands of these and as often as not, after analyzing the questions in hand, sent replies in his own execrable scrawl. His patience and probity, his sheer hard work, to say nothing of his generosity of spirit, combined, what with his influence in Yorkshire, Nottinghamshire, and above all in Sussex, to make him an indispensable leader in the days before the advent of party machines.

He was not, until he succeeded his brother, Henry Pelham, at the Treasury in 1754, the contriver of the government's majorities in Parliament, but where Sussex affairs were concerned, Newcastle made the decisions.[73] Here on the canvas of Sussex he best knew how to paint, and most enjoyed painting, majorities composed in so far as possible of his 'friends'. Most likely some irresistible urge drove him to spend his great fortune so lavishly on politics and with such disinterestedness. To serve one's friends was then expected from a gentleman of rank and employments under the Crown. New-

73. Richmond to Newcastle, 2 Jan. 1746/7: 32710, fol. 5; Owen, *The Rise of the Pelhams,* p. 317.

castle must have felt that to be so laboriously attentive to details and the niceties of human relationships down in Sussex would give him needed reputation, actual or presumptive. He must have needed, even if by means of the baldest flattery received, to persuade himself that he had weight of character because he never quite succeeded in convincing his male intimates—except for Richmond—that he did possess character; and as for dignity, why, spiteful people like Hervey and Horace Walpole thought him a clown. How reassuring it was to receive a letter from an applicant for favors who wrote, 'My Lord, It is a known attribute of your greatness to take a pleasure in supporting these creatures of your own making who profess, as I do and ever shall, an entire duty, devotion, and gratitude to your Grace'.[74] How comforting the verses:

> Then fill your glass. Full let it be
> NEWCASTLE drink while you can see.
> With heart and voice, all voters sing
> Long live great HOLLES—Sussex KING.[75]

Such praises compensated Newcastle for his fear of people. So did his Sussex estates, which, like those of the Duke of Dorset, were scattered over a good deal of East Sussex; in fact, Newcastle's straggled from the borough of Lewes twenty-five miles eastward to include another parliamentary borough, Hastings, which at this time he appears to have managed for the Treasury. At Lewes he leased a mansion in the High Street and turned it into a political club and coffee house to promote the Whig-Pelham interest.[76] Of his three houses in eastern Sussex, Newcastle made Halland, a big Elizabethan pile in the parish of East Hoathly, near Lewes, his principal residence when he visited his cherished county.

74. George Jackson to Newcastle, 3 Feb. 1741/2: 32699, fol. 46.
75. Add. MSS, 32698, fol. 82.
76. Walter H. Godfrey, 'Newcastle House, Lewes', *S.A.C.*, 92 (1954), 3–16.

From Halland Newcastle dispensed his plentiful feastings and the mostly impalpable dew of his influence. What, for Newcastle, was influence? It meant his ducal prestige and his large properties; for example, those houses at Lewes, from which the tenants might be evicted if they voted for Opposition candidates; a network of diligent agents throughout the county: relatives, squires, clergy including Hargraves and Ball, and lesser men, who arranged the little contracts of honor between themselves as the Duke's representatives and the voters and who knew so intimately the circumstances of Sussex politics that they could foretell the numbers of votes on each side in a contest with astonishing accuracy. Influence meant diplomacy: Newcastle must sense the point beyond which a borough patron was unwilling to go in obliging him, the moment when such an informal alliance was reached or broken and the causes of the breach; above all, Newcastle could not afford to be, like the 'proud' Duke of Somerset at Petworth, aloof. He must know the littlest men. There is substantial truth in Horace Walpole's cock-and-bull story that Newcastle, while reviewing English troops at Nestleroy in 1748, 'hurried about with his glass up to his eye, crying, "Finest troops! finest troops! greatest general!" then broke through the ranks when he spied any Sussex man, kissed him in all his accoutrements, "My dear Tom such an one!" [and] chattered of Lewes races'.[77] Newcastle had need to know as many voters as he could in the county of Sussex and in its thirteen parliamentary boroughs.

Next to Cornwall, Wiltshire, and Yorkshire, Sussex in these unreformed days sent more representatives to Westminster than any other county in England—twenty-eight.[78] There

77. Horace Walpole to Horace Mann, Mistley, 14 July 1748. *The Yale Edition of Horace Walpole's Correspondence,* ed. W. S. Lewis, *19,* 495.

78. For analyses of the franchises and state of representation in both the county and the thirteen boroughs of Sussex see, for 1741, Nadel, 'The Sussex Election of 1741'; for 1754–1790, Sir Lewis Namier and John Brooke, *The House of Commons, 1754–1790* (3 vols. published for the History of Parliament Trust by Her Majesty's Stationery Office,

were two members for the county and two each for Arundel, Bramber, Chichester, the Duke of Dorset's East Grinstead, Horsham, Lewes, Midhurst, New Shoreham, Steyning, and the four Cinque Ports within the county—the 'ancient towns' of Rye and Winchelsea, Hastings, and its 'limb', Seaford. There were about 4,000 freeholders in the county; Chichester had about 530 voters in 1733;[79] in 1741 Lewes had over 200,[80] New Shoreham some 130, and Bramber and East Grinstead 36 each.[81] The tiny groups of electors in Sussex boroughs, with the probable exception of the Chichester voters, languished morally and throve materially under the soiled hands of patrons.

Newcastle's ability to attract the voters of Sussex varied with his own and his agents' diligence, with his being in or out of favor at Court, with the indifference of thirst and greed of voters, with the tempers of independents, especially with the electoral strength of his allies among the dukes and other important landowners of Sussex. Grow his influence did from its origins back in 1715, when George I made him a duke, but it would be hazardous to assume that his power rose steadily to a culmination at the end of his life in 1768. The period of his greatest authority in Sussex reached from the general election of 1734 to his fall from office in 1762. In 1741, to judge by the results of the general election in that year, Newcastle's party in the House of Commons was numerous if in size not unusual. The group numbered just after the election sixteen 'immedi-

---

London, 1964); for the autumn of 1762, 'Report of the State of Elections, Sussex', Stowe Papers (uncatalogued), Henry E. Huntington Library and Art Gallery; for the early nineteenth century, T. H. B. Oldfield, *The Representative History of Great Britain and Ireland* (London, 1816), 5, 1–61, 373–87, 404–72; and J. Holladay Philbin, *Parliamentary Representation, 1832, England and Wales* (New Haven, privately printed, 1965), pp. 187–200.

79. Richmond to Newcastle, Goodwood, 2 Aug. 1733: 32688, fol. 41.
80. Newcastle to his wife, Lewes, 2 May [1741]: 33073, fol. 178.
81. Nadel, 'The Sussex Election of 1741', pp. 108, 110, 116.

ate relatives and personal dependents'.[82] Of these, nine represented constituencies outside Sussex and are therefore irrelevant. Seven only, out of some twenty-two returned in the interest of the Court from Sussex,[83] were the Duke's own men —his private secretary, four more or less distant relatives, his brother Henry, and Henry's partner in the representation of the county, James Butler. (Yet what prodigious labors were necessary to secure the elections of these seven!) Two only, the members for Lewes, 'owed their election to the Duke in his private capacity'; three owed their seats at Hastings and Seaford either to his management of these boroughs for the Treasury or to the Crown.[84] That Henry Pelham and Butler should have swept the county was due as much to Newcastle's understandings with his Sussex allies as to his own influence—influence that was defined by the freeholders' own motives in supporting his candidates: fear, self-interest, incapacity to oppose, regard for the tradition of having a Pelham represent the county, and (let the triumph be judged in part by Newcastle's popularity) sheer good will.[85] Quite impalpable was the degree of his political influence over his friends Thomas Archer at Bramber, Richmond at Chichester, Dorset at East Grinstead, Colonel Ingram at Horsham, and Sir William Gage at Seaford. Of no little service in the return of friendly members from Chichester and in the support given by freeholders, particularly in western Sussex,[86] was Newcastle's felted grip on the Bishop, the Dean and Chapter (with the exception of Canon Parke), the Precentor, Chancellor, Treasurer, and on the remaining prebendaries of Chichester.

82. Owen, *The Rise of the Pelhams,* p. 46. Owen gives the number as fifteen. The sixteenth was James Butler, M.P. for Sussex, who died ten days after the election.

83. Nadel, 'The Sussex Election of 1741', p. 87.

84. Owen, *The Rise of the Pelhams,* p. 46 and nn. 2, 3.

85. See Sir Lewis Namier, *The Structure of Politics at the Accession of George III* (2d ed. London, Macmillan, 1957), pp. 143–44.

86. Richmond in 1741 estimated that Chichester contained 204 freeholders. Richmond to Newcastle, Goodwood, 15 July 1741: 32697, fol. 317.

The measure of a man's worth can sometimes be taken from the friends he makes and keeps. Few of Newcastle's relationships with the men of his times do him such bright honor as the devotion of Charles Lennox, second Duke of Richmond. 'To you, and you only,' Richmond wrote to him after years of intimacy, 'I open my heart, knowing it is to the best and dearest friend I have in the world.'[87] 'There never lived a man,' Lord Hervey confessed of Richmond in a moment of rare charity, 'of a more amiable composition: he was friendly, benevolent, generous, honourable, and thoroughly noble in his way of acting, talking, and thinking; he had constant spirits.'[88] Hervey's opinion is amply borne out (except perhaps for the 'noble' behavior) by those wonderfully unguarded letters to Newcastle, into which Richmond was wont to pack his horse sense, his sizing up of men, his humor, and so much of his affection. He had, of course, many honors: besides the English dukedoms of Richmond and Lennox, which he had inherited in 1723 from his father, one of Charles II's bastards, he was Duc d'Aubigny in the peerage of France, Master of the Horse, Brigadier-General, Captain of the Blues, Knight of the Garter, President of the Society for the Encouragement of Learning, and so on, a list appropriately ducal and one that altogether hid the exuberantly English squire Richmond always was. He had been born in 1701 at Goodwood, and here he loved to live his days. Why not? The country, he said, was 'most delightful'. What better sport than frightening Canon Sherwin almost to death? The Goodwood party hated Dr. Sherwin.[89] In the summer of 1733, shortly after Sherwin had without permission published Lord Hervey's attack on Pope, Richmond was out on the Downs quite literally after Sherwin's wits. With his

87. Richmond to Newcastle, Wednesday night [docketed 10 Sept. 1746]: 32708, fol. 249.

88. John, Lord Hervey, *Some Materials towards Memoirs of the Reign of King George II*, ed. Romney Sedgwick (London, King's Printers, 1931), *I*, 252.

89. The Earl of March, *A Duke and His Friends* (London, 1911), *I*, 242.

valet as companion he staged a bogus holdup of his duchess' chaise, in which Sherwin was riding. ' "Dam ye, the booty," says I . . . "Dam ye," say I, "your gold and your watch" . . . *slap* I lett fly my pop . . . butt the sluggs whistled pretty close by his ears.'[90] As if to restore balance to his activities, Richmond's eminent patronage of Canaletto extended over a period of more than twenty years.[91]

Richmond had grown up and been educated in the hunting field: he would rather hunt on the morrow than meet Newcastle about politics at Bishopstone; he much preferred being with his family to 'fiddle-fadle waiting' at Court;[92] he wished that he had the talent of explaining himself better; and he salted his scribbling with stableyard English. For many years he was master and sole proprietor of the hunt at Charlton in the valley north of the Goodwood hills, the Melton Mowbray of the eighteenth century. In the immortal chase of 26 January 1738/9 he found the fox in Eastdean wood at a quarter before eight in the morning, pursued it through Puntice Coppice to the Marlowes, to Nightingale bottom and Cobden's pinepit hanger (there the Duke of St. Albans got a fall), raced through 'my Lady Lewkner's buttocks', and on to West Dean forest, to Collar Down 'where Lord Harcourt blew his first horse', drove cross by Cocking course, down between Graffam and Woolavington to the Hurlands, Selham, Amersham, over Totham heath almost to Cowdray Park only to climb the hills between Bepton and Cocking. 'Here the unfortunate Lord Harcourt's second horse felt the effect of long legs and a sudden steep, the best thing belonging to him was his saddle which my Lord had secured, but by bleeding and Geneva[93] (contrary to the Act of Parliament) he recovered, and with

90. The Earl of March, *A Duke and His Friends*, *1*, 266–67.

91. Hilda F. Finberg, 'Canaletto in England', *The Ninth Volume of the Walpole Society* (1920–21), pp. 21–54. W. G. Constable, *Canaletto* (2 vols. Oxford, Clarendon Press, 1961).

92. Richmond to Newcastle, 28 Nov. 1742: 32699, fol. 540.

93. A spirit resembling gin.

some difficulty got home;' galloped on through the warren above West Dean, where he dropped Sir Harry Liddel, on down to Binderton Farm ('here Lord Harry sunk'), through Goodwood Park and furiously up to Strettington Road, by Sally Coppice, where he himself got a 'somerset', to Kemp's high wood; finally in the winter dusk he reached the wall of Arundel river. Here 'the Glorious Twenty Three Hounds putt an end to the Campaign, and killed the Old Bitch Fox, 10 minutes before six. Billy Ives, His Grace of Richmond, and B[rigadie]r Hawley were the only Persons at the Death.'[94] Thus Richmond wrote in his journal. His taste for sport did not end with hunters and hounds. He was among the first gentlemen to organize cricket matches in Sussex.[95] He kept behind iron bars in Goodwood dens '5 woulves, 2 tygerrs, 1 lyon, 2 lepers, a jack all, 3 bears, a woman tygerr, 3 racoons, 7 caseawarris'.[96] Newcastle sent him a buffalo cow.[97]

The zoo may have suggested eccentricity. Richmond's steadfast convictions proclaimed the virtues of a country gentleman. He was one of those aristocrats in whom England has been fortunate beyond any other nation: taking his position for granted, yet so using it and his wealth as to be of aid to his community, he brought, as Burke might have said of him, the dispositions that are lovely in private life into the service and conduct of the commonwealth. The elementary principles by which he lived, his humor, which always he kept half-turned upon his own conduct, no less than his hunting helped him to see his world at it was; and as hunting led to knowing his hunt servants, Tom Johnson, Tom Leaver, Joe Budd, Will Macey, Billy Ives, and David, and knowing his hunt servants

94. The Earl of March, *Records of the Old Charlton Hunt* (London, 1910), pp. 62–64.

95. H. F. and A. P. Squire, *Henfield Cricket and Its Sussex Cradle* (Hove, 1949), pp. 33–40.

96. The Earl of March, *A Duke and His Friends*, 1, 138–39.

97. Richmond to Newcastle, Charlton, 24 Nov. 1734: 32689, fol. 495.

to knowing the countryside, and to understanding how men live and how they are to be persuaded (a science pleasanter by far and subtler too than Chesterfield's), Richmond came to know what could be expected of 'Tanky', of that 'old fool' the Duke of Somerset, and of the respectable if slightly pretentious folk at Chichester—'Sir Jon' Miller, 'Lisbon' Peckham, the Bishop, the Dean, and the kit-and-boodle of prebendaries. He had, he once said, been 'bred up from a child in Whig principles'.[98] He was a most loyal and disinterested servant to the first two Georges, performing a duty rarely easy to fulfill, and 'thoroughly zealous for both the Government and the Administration'.[99] His character rang true. 'I never can', he told Newcastle, forgetful of his grammar, 'nor never will *vote* against my principles, which I am farr from being ashamed of.'[100] He did not spare words in censuring moral weakness when it might hurt king and country whom it was the first of his duties to serve.[101] For all his jesting he could be implacable as a Lord Justice in bringing murderous smugglers to the gallows.[102] Jobbery he despised. 'By the word *job* I understand aplying the publick money to private uses; which in my opinion is villany.'[103] His saving laughter might have prompted him to put a name to the practice of applying private money to public uses like vote catching, except that most of his friends did just that, and he himself in 1733 had not only been at 'expence amongst the freeholders' in and around Chichester[104] but had assured Newcastle that he looked upon the borough of New Shoreham 'as a new whore,

98. Richmond to Newcastle, Hanau, 29 June/10 July 1743. The Earl of March, *A Duke and His Friends, 2,* 412.

99. Hervey, *Memoirs of Reign of George II, 1,* 251–52.

100. Richmond to Newcastle, Goodwood, 7 May 1746: 32707, fol. 155.

101. Ibid., 4 June 1746: 32707, fols. 280–83.

102. The Earl of March, *A Duke and His Friends, 2,* 573–96.

103. Richmond to Newcastle, Goodwood, 7 Aug. 1745: 32705, fol. 20.

104. Thomas Ball to Isaac Maddox, Chichester, 3 Oct. 1733: 32688, fol. 448.

that is anybodys for their mony'.[105] He was nothing if not candid.

Goodwood, for all Richmond's *'rantum scantum'* of guests and alarming debts,[106] gave him what he called 'a natural interest' at Chichester.[107] He had sat for the city in 1722/3 and thereafter nominated a succession of kinsmen for one of the seats, while by agreement the other was left at the disposal of independent voters; or, as a committee of citizens later reminded the third Duke of Richmond in 1790, the city had been wont to pay the Duke's family the compliment 'of permitting it to recommend one Member . . . upon the implied condition that we should be undisturbed in the choice of the other'.[108]

Newcastle's shrewdness, as far back as 1723, had caused him to sense Richmond's capacity. Here, he reasoned, might be a valuable ally in western Sussex. He made his decision no more than ten days after Charles Lennox had succeeded his father in the dukedom of Richmond. 'All our friends here . . .' he wrote to Bishop Bowers, 'think we should espouse the Duke of Richmond's interest as being the most solid support of the

105. Richmond to Newcastle, Goodwood, 5 Aug. 1733: 32688, fol. 47. For Richmond's concern for his 'interest' at New Shoreham see The Earl of March, *A Duke and His Friends, 1*, 277–82; also his letters to Sir Robert Walpole, 1733–34, University Library, Cambridge, Cholmondeley Correspondence, 2084, 2095, 2097, 2396a and 68, item 39.

106. Duchess of Richmond to Richmond, Tunbridge Wells, ?1733: Goodwood MSS, Box 25.

107. Richmond to Martin ffolkes, Hampton Court, 11 Oct. 1733: The Earl of March, *A Duke and His Friends, 1*, 259.

108. 'Proposals Made to the Duke of Richmond, 9 Apr. 1790,' Courtesy of L. C. G. Holden, Chichester. *Victoria History of the County of Sussex, 3* (London, 1935), 99–100. In the general election of 1780 the third Duke of Richmond controlled both seats at Chichester, 'though his hold on the second seat was somewhat precarious'—Ian R. Christie, *The End of North's Ministry, 1780–1782* (London, Macmillan, 1958), p. 58. See Sir Lewis Namier and John Brooke, *The House of Commons, 1754–1790, 1*, 390–92.

Whigg interest in Chichester. I therefore conclude you will give your interest to' the young Duke's candidate for the city of Chichester, 'which certainly is right for us to do upon all accounts as the Duke of Richmond is a growing young man and may be very considerable in your parts.'[109]

Events proved Newcastle right. In 1735, and again ten years later, Richmond was Mayor of Chichester. He captured the city's Common Council, a prize which the dukes of Richmond still enjoyed on the eve of the Municipal Corporations Act of 1836.[110] He came, he confessed, to be as fond of Chichester 'as the Duke of Newcastle is of Lewes, 'tho with much more reason'.[111] In 1747 he gained control of the Corporation of Arundel,[112] and succeeded old Somerset as High Steward of Chichester. He was wont, moreover, to recommend candidates for posts in the Church and in the civil service there. He asked of Newcastle the first vacancy as surgeon in St. Thomas's Hospital for a son of Thomas Baker, chandler in Chichester, 'cheif pillar of the Dissenters in these parts', and a man of 'most exceeding good interest both in town and country';[113] and his duchess, to further the interest of her 'dear angel', was willing to attend Westhampnett Church near the park gates and outsit and mightily commend a two-hour sermon preached by 'a mad Welch enthusiast, a sort of Whitfeild . . . a very noisy fellow and mostly followed by the people here, so though he is a sad dog, it would be right to have him, for he can be very serviceable'.[114] Richmond liked his patronage in and around Chichester, even if he knew that ultimately he must defer to Newcastle's wishes.[115] No matter if out of affabil-

109. Newcastle to Bowers, Claremont, 6–7 June 1723: 32686, fol. 253.
110. *Victoria History of the County of Sussex, 3,* 99.
111. Richmond to Dorset, Goodwood, [10 June] 1741: Sackville MSS, County Record Office, Maidstone, Kent.
112. Richmond to Newcastle, Goodwood, 2 Oct. 1747: 32713, fol. 205.
113. Ibid., 8 Sept. 1738: 32691, fols. 343–44.
114. Ibid., 30 July 1740: 32694, fol. 367.
115. Ibid., 14 June 1741: 32697, fol. 190.

ity he insisted that he had the Duke's 'friendship much more at heart than the Church of England'.[116] He nursed the welfare of each.

Suddenly, in October 1741, the Sussex interest of both Newcastle and Richmond was precipitated into full activity. The Dean of Chichester was certainly dying; an accommodating successor must be found; a spate of letters from clerical beggars like Walter Barttelot might be expected. In the midst of all these difficulties Newcastle and Richmond had on their hands a contested by-election for the county. They could not escape the consequences of the union that Whigs had made: the State expected and the Church must assist. And now, as so often before and as things would be again, the links and loops of connection showed their toughness, showed that they could not lightly be undone and that they restricted the freedom of movement of both dukes. It was necessary to walk warily and to hold in one's head so much familiarity with who knew whom in Sussex, who could be counted on, who not, the arts of yielding to pressure and of subtracting an obligation to one man in order to repay a debt to one of more weight. In truth, Newcastle and Richmond found themselves confronted with the matted web of Sussex kith and kin. In the days ahead they met responsibilities of almost inconceivable import and complexity. They needed all their knowledge of Sussex people and all their alertness and diplomacy, so rapidly did little events occur upon the news of Hargraves' likely demise as well as upon a contest for the county itself now blowing up out of the east.

116. Richmond to Newcastle, Goodwood, 19 Sept. 1746: 32708, fol. 339.

TWO. THE BY-ELECTION

UNDER THE TERMS of the Septennial Act another general election had swung round in the spring of 1741. Walpole's power was in decline; against his better judgment the nation had argued itself into war with Spain; and European states were tumbling into the War of the Austrian Succession. Two years before, Admiral Vernon had won his victory before Porto Bello. But now the war dragged on in indecision and delays. In the autumn of 1740 Richmond from the Downs above Goodwood watched frantically as the spire of Chichester Cathedral pointed straight across land to Sir Chaloner Ogle's squadron at Spithead as if to rebuke him for his repeated failures to sail for the West Indies.[1] But the voters appeared to show little concern over the conduct of either national or imperial affairs. Their mental horizons were bounded by their physical confines: by eastern or western Sussex—even by their parishes. No matter. They were willing enough to plunge into the delirium of local elections. Newcastle's agents had already laid plans to entice them. His Grace was taking few chances. In 1734 the contest for Lewes had been close, and the contest for the county hot; the Duke and his friends, according to the defeated Opposition candidate for the county, were said to have spent at least £10,000 on the election, possibly twice that sum.[2] Newcastle's own election bills and payments from July 1733 to the following May had totaled £3608/12/2.[3] His supporters had at the time cried 'Pelham and Butler forever' (in truth there had seemed little reason why his brother, Henry Pelham, and James Butler should not represent the county forever), while their opponents, Sir Cecil Bisshopp of Parham

1. The Earl of March, *A Duke and His Friends, 1,* 337 ff.

2. John Fuller to [Rose Fuller], 11 June 1734: Fuller MSS, 'Letter Book, 1728–1755', Sussex Archaeological Society, Barbican House, Lewes.

3. Add. MSS, 33058, fols. 343–44.

The Right Honorable Henry Pelham. By Isaac Gosset. From the collection of the late Admiral The Honorable Sir Herbert and Lady Meade-Fetherstonhaugh, of Uppark.

and John Fuller of Brightling, were cheered with popular negatives: 'No excise and no dragoons!' Now, six years later, Newcastle, remembering the cost of that election, was anticipating 'a very warm contest'. Only the ghost of a contest showed.

Perhaps Opposition was feeling impoverished. Certainly it was feeling discouraged. Sir Cecil Bisshopp had computed the chances of his election and declined to stand. At Chichester Canon John Parke and 'Lisbon' Peckham of Pallant House were saying that Bisshopp had 'deserted their cause'. Young, ignorant Samuel Medley of Buxted Place would indeed venture to stand, and Opposition hoped to join with him as a candidate Sir John Peachey of West Dean, near Chichester. Sir John consulted a friend and also his family; quickly he became discouraged; he too declined the nomination.[4] Whereupon Medley went about bleakly visiting towns, fairs, and cricket matches during the summer and autumn, asking for himself singly as against Henry Pelham's running mate, Butler. Medley succeeded only in so far as he kept Newcastle's agents guessing, for he failed badly in the art of moist applications: at Midhurst, where Peachey had influence and introduced him, he shocked many persons by giving some twenty members of the grand jury a mere guinea for drink;[5] at Hastings in 1733 the experienced mayor had thought proper to bestow twenty guineas upon the Corporation.[6] In the event, Medley fizzled out just before the election in May 1741 by dying of smallpox.[7]

4. Sir John Peachey to Sir Cecil Bisshopp, Newgrove, 28 Aug. 1740: Parham Papers, 57, 'Letters, 1708–1921', Addenda, Add. 206, 16. John Jewkes to Newcastle, Petworth, 3 Sept. 1740: 32694, fol. 571.

5. Thomas Ball to Newcastle, Chichester, 23 Jan. 1740/1: 32696, fol. 42.

6. Basil Williams, 'The Duke of Newcastle and the Election of 1734', *English Historical Review, 12* (1897), 476.

7. Robert Burnett to Andrew Stone, Halland, 6 April 1741; and Thomas Stonestreet to Thomas Pelham, Lewes, 24 April 1741: 32696, fols. 285, 361.

Miserable youth! Medley had sufficed to set off a little train of explosives, enough to disturb Goodwood and Halland and to bring to the surface oddments of Opposition wreckage. At Chichester that old hand at opposition, 'Lisbon' Peckham, was distributing Medley's circular letters; Richmond's near neighbor, the Countess of Derby, had promised Medley her support, and encouragement was given by Bisshopp and Sir John Peachey. Sir John sat for Midhurst, where he had an interest and where his lord, the Duke of Somerset, had considerable control. To have the lord of the manor of Petworth opposed to James Butler could possibly mean a brush fire of Opposition racing north seven miles to the borders of Surrey among the Duke of Somerset's tenants[8] as well as clergymen who would not stir without his commands.[9]

The 79-year-old Duke of Somerset was a great figure not only in Sussex but in England. He had been a true-blue Revolution Whig in 1688. At the death of Anne he had had the courage of his principles and aided both Argyll and Shrewsbury in securing the Protestant Succession. Marriage to the heiress of the Percys had brought him vast estates including Alnwick, Syon, Northumberland House, and Petworth; the arrest of his son-in-law, the Tory leader Sir William Wyndham, as a Jacobite suspect in the rising of 1715 brought him fury and dudgeon. He soon retired to Petworth for good, wrapping himself in a Whig mishmash of his own: the old man wanted to preserve the ideals of his youth—fundamental rights of the subject rather than the privileges of Parliament;[10] he admired 'the fundamentall principles of the true old Whiggs in former times when the libertys and the propertys

8. John Jewkes to Newcastle, Petworth, 4 May 1734: 32689, fol. 218. Lord Leconfield, *Petworth Manor in the Seventeenth Century* (London, Oxford University Press, 1954), p. 45.

9. Jewkes to Newcastle, Petworth, 25 July 1740: 32694, fol. 300.

10. G. H. Guttridge, *English Whiggism and the American Revolution* (Berkeley and Los Angeles, University of California Press, 1942), pp. 11–12.

44

of the People were their chiefest care',[11] and when there were
no Walpoles and Newcastles to sap the independence of freeholders. He cherished, like many men in the eighteenth century, the idea of neighborhood: he was loyal to his intimates,
to Bulstrode Peachey Knight, his member for Midhurst
(d. 1736),[12] and to his neighbor, Sir Cecil Bisshopp of Parham, whom, were he to offer himself to the county, Somerset
would never desert for James Butler. Butler, he thought, had
served long enough at Westminster and should yield to 'more
ancient familys in our county'.[13] Somerset's one modern notion seems to have been his wish that Sussex bosses would
imitate the practice of other counties in order to cut expenses
and arrange a compromise whereby a Whig and a 'Tory'
represented Sussex.[14]

To offset these really negligible signs of opposition and to
make a glorious show of Whig solidarity Newcastle devised a
meeting of all his principal friends at Horsham early in August
1740 during the assizes. He invited some 230 guests: baronets,
esquires, gentlemen, and 'all the clergy that voted for us the
last time'.[15] Newcastle and Richmond went; Dean Hargraves

11. Somerset to Hardwicke, Petworth, 24 July 1740: Philip C. Yorke,
The Life and Correspondence of Philip Yorke, Earl of Hardwicke (Cambridge, Cambridge University Press, 1913), *1*, 242.

12. Somerset to Richmond, Newmarket, 25 Nov. 1735: Goodwood MSS,
Box 29.

13. Yorke, *Hardwicke, 1,* 242. Somerset to Newcastle [July 1740]:
32694, fol. 294. Somerset to Lord Hardwicke, 24 July 1740: 35586, fols.
263–64.

14. A Northamptonshire man wrote in 1806: 'By the peace of the
county I understand the uninterrupted harmony of its present state of
society, leaving unbroken old family connections and friendships, tenants
without this distressing risque of offending their landlords, and tradesmen
of losing valuable customers in opposite interest.' Keith Grahame Feiling,
The Second Tory Party, 1714–1832 (London, Macmillan, 1938), p. 7.
R. J. Robson, *The Oxfordshire Election of 1754* (London, Oxford University Press, 1949), p. 16 and n. 1.

15. Clarence Perkins, 'Electioneering in the Eighteenth Century',
Quarterly Journal of the University of North Dakota, 13 (1922–23), 107.

and other clerks engaged to attend, and the loyal 'Tanky' (Lord Tankerville) wrote that he would fail 'neither in person nor in venison'.[16] It was not surprising that Newcastle, a few days after the event, should again try to woo the incalculable Sir John Peachey by assuring him that Henry Pelham and Butler had been 'unanimously agreed to' as candidates for the county. He added, by way of encouragement to Sir John, that the Horsham meeting consisted of 'a greater number of considerable gentlemen and persons of distinction than ever was known upon the like occasion'.[17] Another meeting of Newcastle's friends occurred at Lewes races the same month. Eventually Pelham and Butler were returned for the county on May 6, 1741, unopposed. Ten days later James Butler's son wrote urgently to Newcastle, 'This morning at half after ten was my father's fatal minute'.[18] James Butler had also died of smallpox,[19] and Sussex was faced with a by-election..

Hastily the Whig magnates took counsel with one another. Newcastle suggested to Lord Wilmington that the latter's great-nephew, Charles Sackville, styled Earl of Middlesex, should stand in Butler's place. Wilmington, whose estate lay near Eastbourne in the eastern division of Sussex, took the matter up with the young man's father, the Duke of Dorset.[20] Here likewise connection played its part. Newcastle and Dorset had been political associates for many years, and Dorset worked intimately with his uncle, Spencer Compton, who had sat for Dorset's borough of East Grinstead between 1713 and 1722, served as Speaker of the House (1715–27), and in 1730

16. Clarence Perkins, 'Electioneering in the Eighteenth Century, *Quarterly Journal of the University of North Dakota, 13,* 107.

17. Newcastle to Sir John Peachey, Newcastle House, 9 Aug. 1740: 32694, fol. 434. William Albery, *A Parliamentary History of the Ancient Borough of Horsham* (London, 1927), pp. 84–85.

18. John Butler to Newcastle [16 May 1741]: 32697, fol. 3.

19. Newcastle to his wife, Newcastle House, 14 May 1741: 33073, fol. 180 (Butler very ill with smallpox; little hope of his recovery).

20. Wilmington to Newcastle, Chiswick, 24 May 1741: 32697, fol. 76.

was created Earl of Wilmington and made Lord President of the Council.[21]

Indeed, as far back as 1722, the uncontested election for the county of Sussex had neatly displayed the alliance between the Dukes of Newcastle and of Dorset. At the same time, the occasion had also displayed not only the hierarchical structure of political association but what has been called civilian feudalism, based as that feudalism still was upon land and loyalty to a patron; or, to elaborate, the phenomenon had become a pallid simulacrum of Tudor maintenance and liveried retaining—an institutional palimpsest suggesting a probable origin for eighteenth-century political connections or parties.[22] No men attired in plate armor and bearing swords and lances, no men whose military character had been softened during the sixteenth century into velvet, damask, and javelins,[23] entered Lewes on that April day in 1722. But men, some steps removed from armed retainers, yet owing suit and service for favors past and future, did. About eleven in the morning Spencer Compton came to the top of Glyndebourne Hill near Lewes, accompanied by the head of his family in Sussex, his nephew Dorset, 'and a very great number of clergy, gentlemen, and freeholders'. Soon after, Compton was joined by the other candidate for the county, Henry Pelham, who was himself accompanied by his elder brother, the Duke of Newcastle, 'and a very great appearance likewise of clergy, gentlemen and freeholders'. The two candidates received each other 'with

21. For Dorset's close ties with Wilmington in the thirties, see Hervey, *Memoirs of Reign of George II, 1*, 174–75, *3*, 635; and Chesterfield, *Letters*, ed. Bonamy Dobree (London, Eyre and Spottiswoode, 1932), *1*, 69; *2*, 281.

22. Sir Lewis Namier, *England in the Age of the American Revolution* (2d ed. New York, St. Martin's Press, 1961), p. 8. W. H. Dunham, Jr., 'Lord Hastings' Indentured Retainers', *Transactions of the Connecticut Academy of Arts and Sciences, 39* (1955); Lawrence Stone, *The Crisis of the Aristocracy, 1558–1641* (Oxford, Clarendon Press, 1965), pp. 202–14.

23. Dunham, 'Lord Hastings' Indentured Retainers', p. 115.

mutual acclamations of joy'. Together they proceeded to Lewes in the following order: the gentlemen's servants; the high sheriff's men, holding pikes; the music; the clergy 'in a body which consisted of a greater number than has been known on the like occasion'; the high sheriff himself, attended by six running footmen. There followed Compton and Pelham, 'supported' (what profound implications in that word!) on each side by Dorset and Newcastle. Lastly came the gentlemen and freeholders. In such manner were the two candidates 'cry'd up by the unanimous voice of the county' and elected to Parliament.[24]

Thus, in the spring of 1741, nothing could have been more natural than for three great landowners of eastern Sussex to confer—for the Duke of Newcastle to propose and, with Henry Pelham keeping his brother informed, for the Duke of Dorset to meet with Lord Wilmington three days after Butler's death and to settle upon the Duke of Dorset's eldest son, Lord Middlesex, as their candidate for the county.

Middlesex[25] was a rake. After passing like so many Court Whigs from Westminster School to Christ Church, he sat for his father's pocket borough in Sussex, East Grinstead, in 1734 and again in 1741. His interests, it seems, lay elsewhere than in the House of Commons. In London on the night of January 30, 1734/35, he had got himself into a notorious scrape. He had gone with several companions to the Golden Eagle in Suffolk Street. Here the friends got drunk, and, forgetting that it was the anniversary of the execution of Charles I, they were so indiscreet as to order a bonfire to be lit in the street. A crowd formed. Through its collective head coursed memories of a legend about republicans meeting on that day to dine off a

24. Abel Boyer, *The Political State of Great Britain*, 23, 504, quoted in Nulle, *Newcastle*, pp. 144–46.

25. For Lord Middlesex and something of his part in the contested by-election for the county of Sussex in 1741, see R. L. Hess, 'The Sackville Family and Sussex Politics: The Campaign for the By-Election, 1741', *S.A.C.*, 99 (1961), 20–37.

calf's head. The crowd grew violent. Middlesex and his friends leaned out of the windows to drink the healths of the King, Queen, royal family, Protestant Succession, Liberty, Property, and the present Administration. To no avail. The crowd rioted and wrecked the house; at length a magistrate and the guards arrived.[26] Middlesex went to Italy. He belonged to the Dilettanti. And while he was canvassing Sussex in the summer of 1741, his purse wrestled with his imagination over the operas he would produce in town by mismanaging both his father's money and the subscriptions of his friends.[27] He had just turned thirty.

Newcastle's circle apparently ignored Middlesex's want of steadiness. Their delight in picking him mounted with the arrival of congratulations. But they did show concern over the emergence in western Sussex of prejudice against the selection of another easterner (Henry Pelham, the sitting member, was such) to take the place of Butler, whose estate had lain in the west. Their choice of Middlesex collided with deep local feeling which, underpinning eighteenth-century politics, had caused one of the Duke's members for Aldborough in Yorkshire in 1733 to say that choosing two candidates for the county, both of whom lived in the West Riding, was 'wrong'.[28] Jealousy between the eastern division of Sussex, of which Lewes was the focal center, and the western, where the towers of Chichester cast long political shadows, had existed since the time of William III.[29] The choice of Middlesex disturbed

26. Middlesex to Joseph Spence, Whitehall, 9 Feb. 1734/5: Joseph Spence, *Anecdotes, Observations, and Characters, of Books and Men,* ed. Samuel Weller Singer (London, 1858), pp. 300–05. Henry Benjamin Wheatley, *London, Past and Present* (London, 1930), *s.v.* Suffolk Street.

27. Horace Walpole to Horace Mann, 5 Nov. 1741, 4 May 1743, *The Yale Edition of Horace Walpole's Correspondence,* ed. W. S. Lewis, *17,* 191–92, *18,* 225–26; Charles Burney, *A General History of Music,* ed. Frank Mercer (London, 1935), 2, 817 n., 838, 839, 846, 847.

28. William Jessop to Newcastle, Broomhall, 20 Oct. 1733: 32688, fol. 528.

29. Nulle, *Newcastle,* pp. 32–33.

many a westerner, for the Sackvilles' principal seat was not in Sussex but at Knole, in Kent. 'I believe,' wrote Sir William Gage, an easterner himself, 'we shall meet with some difficulty and some coldness' because Middlesex did not live 'in our county'.[30] Even Newcastle's brother-in-law, Sir John Shelley, who lived near Arundel and who had represented that borough from 1727 to 1741, sidestepped the Duke of Dorset's request that he support Lord Middlesex. He told Dorset that he and some of his friends wished to see the late James Butler succeeded by 'a Western Gentleman' and added that he had no motive other than 'a due Regard to the Interest of that part of the County where I reside'.[31]

Old Somerset was particularly irked by the nomination of Lord Middlesex. He too replied to Dorset's letter asking for his interest. For some years, he wrote, he had been under engagements to his neighbor, the Opposition leader, Sir Cecil Bisshopp, and although content that the eastern division was represented by Henry Pelham, 'a very worthy and Honourable Gentleman', he wished to see a true westerner chosen for his own division.[32] He explained the reason for his views somewhat more clearly to the Duke of Newcastle: in Sussex for more than fifty years there had been a strong and substantial engagement 'always to be for a gentleman of the west, the other for the east, never for both out of the east. . . . it will be very hard upon us western freeholders if we cannot have a gentleman of our own division to supply the western vacancy'.[33] Somerset then temporized. He would, so Richmond heard, be neuter and 'not medle at all';[34] Dorset's agent reported that at Petworth and in neighboring parishes Somerset was getting

30. Gage to Newcastle, 28 May 1741: 32697, fol. 94.

31. Sir John Shelley to Dorset, Michelgrove, 28 May 1741: Sackville MSS, Kent County Record Office, Maidstone.

32. Somerset to Dorset, Petworth, 28 May 1741: Sackville MSS.

33. Somerset to Newcastle, Petworth, 31 May 1741: 32697, fol. 132.

34. Richmond to Dorset, Goodwood [10 June], 16 June 1741: Sackville MSS.

as many freeholders as he could 'not to promise their votes to any one'.[35] But at length, with head untrammeled by logic and with what Richmond called 'the old fool's vain heart' won by flattery,[36] Somerset threw his interest not only to another easterner, but to a leader of the Opposition, Thomas Sergison of Cuckfield near Lewes. (Cuckfield was at least nearer the west than was Knole.) News of Sergison's decision to contest the county deepened anxieties over western prejudice into dread of a strong opponent. It frightened Dorset 'out of his wits': he hoped, Pelham wrote to his brother, 'we will direct him what to do, but says he will spare neither pains nor money'.[37] Dorset had less time now to ponder the cost of his son's operas. An equally lavish entertainment loomed. Everything centered on Lewes. There, on May 23, at 'a pretty large meeting of gentlemen in the opposition at the Star' Sergison was declared a candidate for the county and straightway went about the town asking for votes.[38] Not until June 2 did Newcastle and his friends meet at Lewes, where, with one westerner to propose and another, Sir John Miller, to second, they made Lord Middlesex palatable and unanimously set him up for the county.[39]

Ability of itself did not win elections. In 1734, for example, had the energy and ingenuity sufficed, with which Sergison contested the borough of Lewes, he and his partner might readily have defeated Newcastle's two sluggish cousins. As it was, Sergison came near to winning: he received only thirteen votes less than his victorious Whig opponent.[40] At Lewes, as often in Sussex, ownership of real estate carried elections. The

35. Jonathan Kizzill to Dorset, Goodwood, 12 July 1741: Sackville MSS.

36. Richmond to Newcastle, Goodwood, 11 Aug. 1741: 32697, fol. 409.

37. Henry Pelham to Newcastle, Friday, 9 o'clock [docketed 22 May 1741]: 32697, fol. 45.

38. John Whitfeld to ———, Lewes, 23 May 1741: 32697, fol. 52.

39. Middlesex to the Freeholders of Sussex, 2 June 1741: 32697, fol. 143. Newcastle to his wife, Halland, 3 June 1741: 33073, fol. 182.

40. Williams, 'The Duke of Newcastle', p. 487.

right of election was in the inhabitants, being householders and paying the poor rates. Everything therefore, or almost everything, depended on the appointment of the returning officers, the control of the poor books, and particularly on the lease or ownership of houses within the four parishes. Both sides, pushing occupants in and out, scrambled for houses. A survey of dwellings in two of the parishes showed the Pelhams holding 87 against Sergison's 36 out of a total of 307.[41] More, surely, than a straw in the wind. Newcastle had need to prove himself a good patron there of such craftsmen and tradesmen as carpenters, ironmongers, bricklayers, butchers, the new pastry cook, and the gingerbread baker.[42] He must redress the housing shortage at Lewes by finding a house for a voter to live in; otherwise the man would give his vote to Sergison. Or the Duke must buy a house offered at an exorbitant price or, better still, play the Opposition's own game and evict tenants. The Duke, it had been estimated back in 1734, could turn out eleven of their voters as against their power to toss into the streets no more than three of his.[43]

After his defeat at Lewes in 1734 Sergison did not know his own mind. At that moment he had perhaps been a Tory, doubtless incensed along with the tradespeople of the borough by Walpole's proffered excise. But now, in 1741, although his imputed Toryism may have cooled, he was no less bent upon asserting his independence of any master, most of all a Pelham. Like many other country gentlemen, he much wanted 'to make a considerable figure in his county'[44] by sitting in the House of Commons. Unfortunately for him he was a new man: he lacked the self-assurance that sprang from long-settled

41. List of the Several Houses within the Borough of Lewes, Feb. 1738/39, 32692, fols. 13–16. Cf. 32689, fols. 106–12; *Sussex Notes and Queries, 1* (1926–27), 176–79.

42. Robert Burnett to Andrew Stone, Halland, 6 April 1741: 32696, fol. 285.

43. Williams, 'The Duke of Newcastle', p. 485.

44. William Poole to Newcastle, Hook, 7 Aug. 1746: 32708, fol. 35.

properties like the Barttelots' and the Pelhams'. He came of yeoman stock. He had been born in 1700/01, the son of a mercer of Cuckfield. Through his mother he had inherited Cuckfield Place, the estate of his great-uncle Charles Sergison, 'the old Jew . . . who got his money by opus and usus',[45] presumably as Clerk of the Acts. There followed the restless ambition, those houses at Lewes, which gave him a 'natural interest' in the town,[46] and the need of even more money if he was to carry the county.[47] But as one who studied his moods closely remarked, 'such is the disposition, irresolution, and closeness of the man that with as many hundreds as he has thousands per year, without vanity I could engage to bring more votes to a county election'.[48] He was given to being at sixes and sevens, now vigorously determined to represent Lewes—or should it be the county?—now thinking to be chosen at Steyning,[49] now in retirement, but at all times keeping Newcastle's spies guessing what next he would do.

In late May and during the early summer of 1741 Sergison betrayed no such hesitation. He invaded the west. He stopped with his ally, Sir John Peachey, at West Dean and attended a cricket match at Jemmy Lumley's seat, Stansted Park. The crowd that day at Stansted was enormous—'above 5000 people', Richmond thought. But although Sergison was accompanied by 'Lisbon' Peckham and several more of the Chichester 'Tories', such was the number of ministerial Whigs that Sergison stole away without asking a vote. Perhaps Lord Tankerville was too much for him. Richmond had brought Tanky along to 'swell and look big' and 'puff his cheeks' at

45. Henry Shelley to Newcastle, London, 22 Nov. 1733: 32689, fol. 49.

46. William Poole to Newcastle, Lewes, 10 Dec. 1743: 32701, fols. 306–07.

47. Thomas Pelham to Newcastle, Lewes, Friday morning, Oct. 1740: 32695, fol. 239.

48. Poole to Newcastle, Lewes, 10 Dec. 1743: 32701, fols. 306–07.

49. John Whitfeld to Newcastle, Lewes, 7 Oct. 1740: 32695, fols. 213, 239.

the Opposition candidate.[50] After vainly canvassing Chichester and its neighborhood Sergison turned east.

Meanwhile Lord Middlesex had begun his tour of the county. Quick upon his nomination at Lewes, he and Henry Pelham, like Dante and Virgil, visited the hells of eastern boroughs, winning plaudits, despite the wiser man's reflection that Middlesex was 'not cutt out for this work, but from his excellent good understanding does nothing wrong'.[51] Richmond took charge of the young man's tour of the west and planned his itinerary with care. Middlesex would be received and guided by the principal men within the Pelhams' political structure in Sussex—in turn by Lord Abergavenny of Kidbrook, John Board of Paxhill, Jack Butler of Warminghurst, Sir William Gage of Firle—until Richmond himself picked up the candidate at Petworth and carried him off for further hard work at Goodwood and Chichester. 'Wee have not omitted one necessary place for him to go to', Richmond told Dorset; and he assured the anxious parent that Middlesex would be obliged to entertain his supporters at not more than three places—Petworth, Chichester, and Arundel. Richmond would give a public dinner for him at Goodwood on July 13; at Chichester Lord Middlesex would dine with the Bishop, visit only Dean Hargraves among members of the Chapter, treat some 160 'friends' at the Council House, and be made free of the city. He would also breakfast with John Page, the independent Member for Chichester, spend the night at Tanky's Uppark, dine the next day with Sir John Miller, who had seconded his nomination, return to Goodwood, dine next with Lumley at Stansted, and after passing a night at Arundel Castle cap his vote-catching progress by meeting the Whig

50. Richmond to Newcastle, Goodwood, 16 June 1741: 32697, fol. 202. Richmond to Dorset, Goodwood, 16 June 1741: Sackville MSS.

51. Henry Pelham to Newcastle, Crowhurst, 9 June 1741, and Rye, 12 June 1741: 32697, fols. 164, 175.

magnates in time for the races and assizes at Lewes on the twentieth.[52]

His several sponsors saw to it that Middlesex kept to his schedule. Possibly in their planning they considered what might happen when they thrust the candidate into Sergison's own country at Lindfield. Certainly they did not foresee that Sergison would dare rake up the old Suffolk Street scandal about Middlesex, but Sergison did revive the tale and revived it with gusto. On the day that Middlesex was to be at Lindfield Sergison sent three or four fellows from Cuckfield, bearing in procession a calf's head on the end of a long pole and huzzaing and crying out as they went, and in Sergison's presence too, 'no calves-head clubmen, no Presbyterians'. In their effort to raise a mob they succeeded in provoking only the servant of Newcastle's agent and Middlesex's host, John Board. The servant attacked them, snatched their calf's head, 'beat it about their own ears, and broke one of their heads very handsomely'; for which offense Sergison, it appears, threatened him with the law; whereupon both counsel and attorney offered to defend him gratis. In revenge, Sergison seized the keys of the belfry and church of Board's Paxhill the evening before Middlesex arrived. For counterattack Board had the doors opened and the bells rung; Sergison sent his servant to bribe the ringers to coat the bells so that they could not be heard, and, Whig stalwarts to a man, they answered that from Board's generosity they wished nothing more and would continue, if he wished, to ring as long as they had skin on their fingers.[53]

Among the encouraging, sometimes daily reports of Middlesex's tour to reach Newcastle and Dorset, the Duke of Richmond's showed at first exuberance, then concern, but always confidence in victory. He sent by means of the most appropriate persons upwards of seven hundred circular letters to

52. Richmond to Dorset, Whitehall, 4 July 1741, enclosing Richmond's plan for Middlesex's 'rout': Sackville MSS.

53. Board to Newcastle, Paxhill, 4 July 1741: 32697, fols. 276–77.

freeholders within the rape of Chichester. He knew how most of these would vote, down to a man. To be sure, at Midhurst, where Somerset and Sir John Peachey ruled supreme in 1741, Sergison would 'beat us five to one';[54] but at West Dean, Peachey's own parish, where there were fifteen freeholders, Richmond crowed that he had 'gott two of them certain' and had hopes of two more including the parson, who had reason to support Middlesex since he owed his preferment not to Sir John but to the Dean and Chapter of Chichester.[55] 'Wee are sure in our quarter of 309 to 194,' and he enclosed an analysis of the voters to prove his point.[56] At Chichester Sergison would 'not have forty *coute qui coute,* and then wee beat him four to one, in our good and Loyal Citty'.[57] Comparable reckonings flowed in from many parts of the county. Six months before the election Richmond was 'fully persuaded' that Middlesex would carry Sussex by more than a thousand votes.[58]

Then why, people were asking, did Sergison insist on standing the contest out? Even in friendly Midhurst the freeholders, as early as August, saw his cause as lost and all allowed that they would be 'vastly out-voted in the East, and in the Sea Ports'.[59] Sergison himself, it was known, expected to lose the election by two hundred votes. That he would have a majority in the west, Richmond said, 'is a most stinking lye of his'.[60]

54. Richmond to Dorset, Goodwood, 16 June 1741: Sackville MSS.
55. Ibid. [10 June 1741]: Sackville MSS.
56. Richmond to Dorset, Whitehall, 4 July 1741: Sackville MSS.
57. Ibid.
58. Ibid.
59. Rev. Stephen Unwin to ———, West Meon, 5 Aug. 1741: Sackville MSS. In Kent, Horace Walpole heard the same report. He wrote to Newcastle's nephew, Lord Lincoln, on 13 Sept. 1741: 'I hear there is great opposition making to Lord Middlesex by a Mr. Sergison, who is determined to spend ten thousand pounds, to make them spend twenty.' *The Yale Edition of Horace Walpole's Correspondence,* ed. W. S. Lewis, *30, 20.*
60. Richmond to Newcastle, Goodwood, 15 Sept. 1741: 32698, fol. 46.

Then why did Sergison persist? Was he trying, as the vulgar imagined, to make Newcastle throw away his money so that for every thousand Sergison spent the Duke would be obliged to lavish five or even six times as much on persuasions? Or was Sergison led by a higher strategy? Did he aim to keep the Opposition united so that the next time Newcastle and his friends should set up two candidates for the county, Sergison or some other might wedge in between them, even as poor Medley had tried to do in the last election before death carried him off?

The hopes of spring turned into the apathy of summer and autumn. Farmers were too busy mowing, haying, or harvesting to come in force to the meetings and entertainments arranged by Richmond. Few people attended his public dinner at Goodwood, there being other distractions on that day. Of 156 promises at Chichester, not more than 100 showed up. Still, Richmond was convinced that Sergison could not possibly have 40 out of 204 freeholders there.[61] Sergison, it was rumored, had unaccountably departed into Somersetshire for a visit.[62] The usual applications for favors continued: Thomas Coulstock wanted to be appointed a mounted revenue officer at Hurstpierpoint;[63] Newcastle must procure a lieutenant colonelcy for a friend of Jemmy Lumley's;[64] Newcastle must also get a pardon for a man accused of smuggling and lately dead in Maidstone Gaol, if only to please 'very many in the west of Sussex and some few' around Firle.[65] One fracas only

61. Richmond to Newcastle, Goodwood, 15 July 1741: 32697, fols. 316–17.

62. Thomas Pelham to Newcastle, Crowhurst, 25 Aug. 1741: 32697, fol. 464.

63. Coulstock to Newcastle, 6 June 1741: 32697, fol. 150.

64. Newcastle to Lord Harrington, Whitehall, 31 July 1741: 32697, fols. 378–79, 396, 444.

65. Sir William Gage to Newcastle, 18 Aug. 1741: 32697, fol. 428. For the custom of tampering with the sentences passed on the notorious smugglers of Sussex see Williams, 'The Duke of Newcastle', pp. 470–71.

seems to have punctured the quiet—something like the destroyer-battleship action in the night after Jutland. The cry of calf's head went up on a cricket field after the game was over and was resented by some of Newcastle's friends. Heavy blows were given. Some of the Duke's friends had the worst of the battle at first, but the western cricketers returned to the field with cricket bats and dealt such smart knocks that they carried the victory. Otherwise, as Sir William Gage had written in July and did again in August, 'the country is att this time quieter and better humoured than for this seven years past', 'and your friends are hearty and unanimous'.[66]

66. Gage to Newcastle, 5 Aug. 1741, Firle, 9 July 1741: 32697, fols. 388–89, 295–96.

SUCH WAS the political state of Sussex during the summer and
autumn of 1741. On October 1 Walter Barttelot opened the
preferment-hunting season by addressing himself to the Duke:

> Being informed by my friends at Chichester that the
> dean is in a very dangerous and declining way and that
> several of the clergy are now preparing to address your
> Grace in hopes of succeeding him, I take the liberty
> among the rest thus early to sollicit your favour and
> recommendation in behalf of myself.[1]

Here, then, in the impending vacancy in Chichester Cathedral was a matter requiring delicate attention. Should
Dr. Hargraves die, Newcastle and Richmond would lose a
truly helpful servant. Should Hargraves die before the election, the Dean's own interest, which centered in the city of
Chichester, might suffer from want of directing. Sherlock's
handsome deanery must speedily be so filled as either to reward a party worker or to strengthen ministerial interest by
pitching upon a relative of one of the Sussex peers—someone,
in fine, with the connections of a Lord Middlesex. There could
be, in consequence, little delay in agreeing upon a successor.

Richmond lost no time. He was full of suggestions. On
October 2 he offered his candidate for Newcastle's consideration. The man was Thomas Ball, Archdeacon of Chichester
and a canon residentiary. It would be, he argued, of great
service to their interest to have him. To have anyone else in
the deanery while Ball was alive would, Richmond assured
the Duke, 'very much hurt' his own interest. Ball, it appears,
knew how to threaten Goodwood influence, were he ignored.

1. Barttelot to Newcastle, Rottingdean, 1 Oct. 1741: 32698, fol. 92.

And to fill Ball's canonry in the Chapter, Richmond proposed his own chaplain, 'poor Green'. If Newcastle would urge Green upon his own man, Canon Clarke, Richmond thought he 'could gett' Ball and Backshell to approve Green for residentiary. He ignored the fourth and senior member of the Chapter, John Parke, for whose opinion, given a majority of true friends, Richmond cared not a fig.[2]

At this point the portrait of Thomas Ball, Archdeacon of Chichester, might have been embellished by showing that, among his other attainments, he had in his youth been a considerable traveler; that because he had traveled farther than either of his greatest patrons he therefore knew mankind; and that he could bear comparison with that other ball to which the mother of Roderick Random dreamed she had given birth—an omen taken to mean that her son would be a great traveler.

Such inferences may be drawn from surviving evidence and standard authorities. Certain it is that about the year 1721 a Thomas Ball petitioned the Society for the Propagation of the Gospel. He stated in his petition that he had lived for 'several years' in the colony of New York, had taught school in the city of New York, had come back to England to tend to his affairs, and was now eager to return to teach school in the French settlement of New Rochelle. Again, presumably in 1725, Thomas Ball informed the Venerable Society that he had been appointed a schoolmaster in South Carolina and asked for an allowance to meet his expenses.[3] Ball, accordingly, received the King's Bounty of £20.[4] Gerald Fothergill in *A List of Emigrant Ministers to America, 1690–1811*[5] chose to identify the petitioner Thomas Ball with Thomas Ball, Archdea-

2. Richmond to Newcastle, Goodwood, 2 Oct. 1741: 32698, fol. 94.

3. Library of Congress, Manuscripts Division. Transcripts of the Society for the Propagation of the Gospel, Series A, *15*, 37–38, *19*, 48–49.

4. P.R.O., T53/32, *Money Book, 29 April 1725–11 Sept. 1726*, fol. 145.

5. (London, 1904), p. 12.

con of Chichester. He wrote: 'Ball, Thomas. Carolina, school-master, March 19, 1725–1726. — Money Book, 32–145', then added, 'Son of Lawrence of Eccleston, Lancs; B. A. 1719 (Foster [*Alumni Oxonienses*])'. John Venn in his *Alumni Cantabrigienses* accepted Fothergill's identification. Wherefore the young Thomas Ball of Chichester was a mighty traveler. Alas! To quote Malthus' confident attack on Godwin, 'This beautiful fabric of the imagination vanishes at the severe touch of truth.' The Rev. Thomas Ball of Chichester never went to America: critical dates of his early career, granted his peregrinations to America, do not make sense; Ball could not be in two places at once. Here is the point: the entry in the *Money Book* omits any mention of the father of the petitioner Thomas Ball. Gerald Fothergill, finding in Foster's *Alumni Oxonienses* a Bachelor of Arts (1719) named Thomas Ball, jumped to a convenient, unwarranted conclusion.[6]

The truth about the Rev. Thomas Ball of Chichester happens to be less geographically spacious than Fothergill imagined. Ball, the future archdeacon and canon residentiary of Chichester, was born in 1697/8 in Eccleston, Lancashire, son of Lawrence Ball, a plebeian. Presumably with the favor of the Earl and Countess of Derby, Thomas went up to Oxford in the early spring of 1715/16 and matriculated at Brascnose College, a loyal, impoverished Hanoverian. The University was then in crisis, convulsed by Whig and Tory animosities.[7] Ball, it may be supposed, must have moved with more than a degree of relish through the commotions of faction. In 1719 he received his B.A. Next year he found himself in serious

6. Additional inquiries have so far yielded nothing. Dr. Frederick L. Weis tells me that he finds no mention of a Thomas Ball among his records of colonial clergy in Virginia, the Carolinas, or in the Middle Colonies. A search among MSS. at Fulham Palace Library for evidence of a Thomas Ball's relations with the Society for the Propagation of the Gospel (ca. 1720–25) also yielded nothing.

7. W. R. Ward, *Georgian Oxford, University Politics in the Eighteenth Century* (Oxford, Clarendon Press, 1958).

trouble. The Principal of Brasenose, who happened also to be Vice-Chancellor of the University, was Dr. Robert Shippen, brother of William Shippen, the Jacobite leader in the House of Commons. On March 25, 1720, Dr. Shippen expelled Ball from Brasenose, *'nullius criminis reum et omnino inauditum'*, as Ball's close friend Isaac Maddox recalled many years later.[8] Although at the time of Ball's expulsion he was suspected of heterodoxy,[9] Maddox may have been nearer the truth when he declared that Ball 'had honestly and boldly opposed the leaving out the name of *George,* when they prayed for the King, and had dared to speak justly of King William'.[10] Ball at once appealed to the Visitor of Brasenose, the Bishop of Lincoln, Edmund Gibson. Gibson ordered him restored, and restored Ball was in May 1720.[11]

Thereafter Ball's fortunes improved. In March 1720/21 he was named to one of four exhibitions paid to the poorest sort of Bachelors of Arts at Brasenose.[12] By this time, it appears, he had found for himself three influential patrons, Lord and Lady Derby and that rising Whig prelate, Edmund Gibson, soon to become Bishop of London and Sir Robert Walpole's 'Pope' and unofficial minister of patronage in the Church of England. Ball shortly scampered into Sussex, where Lord and Lady Derby had an estate, Halnaker, adjoining Goodwood.

In deference to custom as enjoyed by the more favored rather than to the letter of the Thirty-second Canon, this now privileged aspirant to the Cloth was ordained deacon, then priest, in two successive weeks of July 1723 and, four days later,

8. Isaac Maddox to Richmond, Hartlebury, 1 Oct. 1746: 32709, fols. 47–48.

9. Thomas Hearne, *Remarks and Collections,* 7 (Oxford Historical Society, 1906), 131.

10. Maddox to Richmond, Hartlebury, 1 Oct. 1746: 32709, fols. 47–48.

11. Hearne, 7, 131.

12. *Brasenose College Register, 1509–1709* (Oxford Historical Society, 1909), p. 296.

was admitted to the vicarage of Boxgrove, near Halnaker and Goodwood, to which living the Derbys had presented him.[13]

At Boxgrove Lady Derby built Ball a parsonage. Ball and the Countess liked each other; they were 'equally remarkable for benevolence and hospitality';[14] and to her husband Ball professed himself to be 'under greater personal obligations than to any man living'.[15] Thus Ball began life in Sussex. But only momentarily. He veered to Cambridge, where he was admitted pensioner at Caius College in 1725/26 and received the degree of Master of Arts that same year.[16] These mighty things having been done, Ball returned to Chichester and, as was his wont, picked up as many patrons as a dog picks up burrs. He made friends with Isaac Maddox, the Prebendary of Eartham, who many years later as Bishop of Worcester would remain solicitous of his welfare. He cultivated Bishop Waddington, as we have seen, and also Waddington's successor, Francis Hare, who made him his domestic chaplain. As befitted a Whig presbyter on the make, Ball settled happily into a career of clerical politics and preferment under Richmond and then under Newcastle. The dates of his promotions in the Church rang the changes of his fortunes:

13. West Sussex County Record Office. Register K (Bowers), fol. 15. Part of Canon 32 reads as follows: 'Not that always every deacon should be kept from the ministry for a whole year, when the bishop shall find good cause to the contrary, but that there being now four times appointed in every year for the ordination of deacons and ministers, there may ever be some time of trial of their behaviour in the office of deacon, before they be admitted to the order of priesthood.' Sir Robert Phillimore, *The Ecclesiastical Law of the Church of England* (London, 1873), *1*, 128; Sykes, *Church and State*, pp. 200–01.

14. The comment of Ball's son-in-law, the poet William Hayley, in *Memoirs of the Life and Writings of William Hayley*, ed. John Johnson (London, 1823), *1*, 109.

15. Ball to Newcastle, Chichester, 3 Oct. 1733: 32688, fol. 445.

16. John Venn, *Biographical History of Gonville and Caius College*, 2 (Cambridge, 1898), 26.

1723, vicar of Boxgrove; 1727, prebendary of Hampstead; 1729/30, in succession to Maddox, prebendary of Eartham; 1732/33, vicar of Eartham; 1735, canon residentiary; 1736, archdeacon of Chichester; 1738, warden of St. Mary's Hospital. And next surely, the deanery?

Ball was a miniature Newcastle. He loved in his heart a Whig Chapter as dearly as the Duke loved a Cabinet of friends. His joys were politics, intrigue, and insinuation; his sorrow, a mad wife. He loved also to see the fine cliché uncoil from his quill onto the paper, the fitting words conveying his so noble or so accommodating sentiment and suggesting the smile he must have worn when contriving how to please: 'my zeal in the common cause'; 'every Sussex freeholder who loves civil and religious liberty and their best support, the Protestant Succession'; 'this mournful occasion' (Ball gave way to no more tender expression upon Dean Hargraves' death). He was, as William Hayley knew, 'an amiable divine, who had received from nature very sprightly talents, with benevolent and convivial hilarity of temper', a man distinguished for 'social pleasantry. He wrote lively verses on private and domestic occasions with facility and grace'.[17] He was not solely moved by love of gaiety and self-interest. He was not all rogue. Richmond found some inner virtue, when he called him a man of irreproachable life and character.[18] Ball had 'suffered' for 'principles' and would not give them up, however skillfully in 1733 he could detach himself from his patron Derby's factious amity with the Sussex Opposition in order to bolster the Whig interest in the county (of which, he told Newcastle in a whispered parenthesis, 'I take your Grace and your family to be the main support').[19]

There is pleasure in offering, there is rapture in receiving, flattery. The Puritan in Newcastle might have prompted him to turn aside the cruder aspects of this staple of his existence.

17. Hayley, *Memoirs, 1*, 33, 108.
18. Richmond to Newcastle, Goodwood, 19 Sept. 1746: 32708, fol. 338.
19. Ball to Newcastle, Chichester, 3 Oct. 1733: 32688, fols. 445–46.

The Reverend Thomas Ball. Artist unknown. In the possession of the Dean and Chapter of Chichester.

Instead he chose to accept it as deference paid to him as head of a great aristocratic house. Besides cutting into this chink in the Duke's moral armor, Ball knew instinctively how to dispel his inefficiency: he would set him an example at once of loyalty and competence by laying at his feet those lengthy, painstaking reports about the electors all over the county;[20] had he not seen in 1734 to the brooming and provisioning of the episcopal palace, attentive to the last detail to Newcastle's comfort and to the good impression his staying there must make? Intending to alarm, he would humbly offer to the Duke Sir Cecil Bisshopp as an example of assiduous electioneering;[21] then, wheeling again into encouragement, urge that John Peckham's vote could be snared by threatening to prick him for sheriff,[22] or ascertain with nicety the moment in the campaign when 'meer and dry applications only' should be reinforced by 'expensive expedients' (to be sure, Ball wished heartily that they might prove otherwise), whenever 'the independency, indifference, or other danger of . . . freeholders render such sweetness absolutely and immediately necessary';[23] and doucely, with eyes on the contentment of the Cloth, he would advise his patron that by allowing the Rev. Edward Stuart, rector of Wiggonholt *cum* Greatham, two tiny parishes near Pulborough, to keep the vicarage of Goring without having to suffer the expenses of a dispensation,[24] '(for the livings are small and the incumbent in low circumstances)', Newcastle could snatch Mr. Stuart from under the nose of his near neighbor Sir Cecil Bisshopp at Parham, and for the future rely upon his 'inviolable attachment to your Grace's

20. See, for example, Ball to Newcastle, Chichester, 4 Nov. 1733: 32689, fols. 9–10.

21. Ibid., 3 Oct. 1733: 32688, fols. 445–46.

22. Ibid., 4 Nov. 1733: 32689, fols. 9–10. Edward Porritt, *The Unreformed House of Commons* (Cambridge, Cambridge University Press, 1909), *1*, 383–84.

23. Ball to Newcastle, Chichester, 21 Sept. 1740: 32695, fols. 113–14.

24. Phillimore, *Ecclesiastical Law, 2*, 1165–67.

interest'.[25] Above all, the Archdeacon excelled in assuaging the effects of one of Newcastle's and Richmond's worst gaffes.

It began innocently enough. Richmond on January 2, 1740, wrote to Newcastle that 'Sir Jon' Miller was thinking of standing at Chichester in opposition to that independent Whig, John Page. Richmond thought the idea good. In the first place, he had persuaded himself that he detested Page. Page was one of those doubtful fellows who had not promised him to attend the ostentatious assemblage of Whigs at Horsham the previous August.[26] And now Page, who must either be deceiving Sir Robert Walpole or be himself the vilest of men, was every day running about Chichester abusing Sir Robert. Richmond probably did not see that Page was, like himself, a man of principle with this difference only: Page was an independent Whig, whilst the Duke of Richmond believed quite honestly that lesser men, especially if they were Whigs, should defer to him. Miller, indeed, would be the better candidate; why, several of Richmond's friends had said that they would vote for him.[27] Four days later Richmond had become uneasy. At Goodwood his infant daughter lay dying of smallpox. In Chichester he had learned that the inhabitants were determined to suffer no breach of the compromise by which he named one of their members while they kept to themselves the free choice of an independent gentleman for the other seat. Richmond again wrote to Newcastle and cautioned him against going to extremes in endorsing Sir John Miller: such must inevitably hurt Newcastle in the county and himself in the city, where Page's interest, being strong and 'outragious', would immediately declare for young Medley in opposition to Pelham and Butler, throw over Richmond's own candidate for Chichester, his uncle Brudenell, and cry for Page singly. In order, therefore, to clear himself from the suspicion of

25. Ball to Newcastle, Chichester, 21 Sept. 1740: 32695, fols. 113–14.
26. Richmond to Newcastle, Goodwood, 27 July 1740: 32694, fol. 325.
27. Richmond to Newcastle, Findon, 2 Jan. 1740/1: 32696, fol. 6.

conspiracy, Richmond the day before had addressed ostensible letters to both the mayor and his own chaplain, Canon Green. In these he expressly detached himself from Sir John. He hoped his friends would see Brudenell's election safe and, bowing to the necessity of admitting the independence of the Chichester voters, declared he thought himself 'highly oblige [d] to the city for allowing him to recommend his uncle, and that he *never* would think of recommending both their members'.[28]

By January 7 catastrophe hit Chichester. It was known that Newcastle had approved Sir John Miller's candidacy. In fact, Newcastle was 'delighted', concluding that Sir John by his proposal offered no threat to Richmond's interest and inclination, and in company at Bishopstone had drunk Sir John's health.[29] Richmond was frantic. He accused Newcastle of too great 'vivacity'. The petard now hoisting their Graces had started 'such a flame as never was seen'. It was, to be sure, not so intense as to demolish the odds on Brudenell, Pelham, and Butler, but it would suffice; Alderman Soane, Page's father-in-law and 'the most zealous friend wee had for the county as well as for the town' (did Richmond's past tense sink home?), had also become 'outragious'; Soane now vowed that if Newcastle should oppose Page, he would do his utmost for Medley and probably quit Brudenell; and several more talked in the same way, and Richmond assured Newcastle that they were a great many, and Newcastle must know that Page had a great interest. Richmond's ostensible letters would save him; but what of Newcastle? Richmond implored his friend to ask Sir John

28. Richmond to Newcastle, Goodwood, 6 Jan. 1740/1: 32696, fols. 11–13. For the intrigues by which Richmond's eldest son and heir, the third Duke, tried to secure the nomination of both seats at Chichester (and he did), see the letter of that Independent, John Page, to Newcastle, Watergate House, 14 Jan. 1767 (32979 fols. 224–25); also Namier and Brooke, *The House of Commons, 1754–1790, 1,* 390–92.

29. Newcastle to Richmond, Bishopstone, 4 Jan. 1740/1: Goodwood MSS, Box 25.

to desist and had already burned Newcastle's letter to Miller. He was now willing to compound for Page in order to throw out Medley. But what a dilemma! He still preferred Sir John, 'because we have a chance for him *gratis*', whereas Page would, if possible, have to be bought even as Richmond bought toys from Mrs. Chenevix. What, moreover, would Sir John's spending £1,000 avail? 'For twice the summe I am very sure he would not come in for Chichester.' Just before Richmond ended his letter someone brought him a note from Sir John Miller announcing his withdrawal from the election.[30]

Sir John Miller, fourth baronet, of West Lavant, near Chichester, had lived all his life in the country. For the moment, wishing to revive his family's tradition, he 'most excessively' wanted to represent Chichester in the House of Commons. He, too, had acquired some interest in that city, and his late aunt had been the wife of Canon Backshell and a relative of the Peacheys of West Dean. Unfortunately Sir John had neither Page's intelligence[31] nor his political experience and independence of mind. Page had in 1720 been a clerk in the South Sea House. He retired to his native Chichester, bought a small estate at Up Marden on the Downs, and from 1727 until 1734 had sat for a borough in Lincolnshire. Now he was offering himself for the city of Chichester, but on his own terms. He supported ministers when he saw fit; he also attacked them. As he told Newcastle in 1758, he had become in consequence of serving near thirty years in Parliament a poorer man by fourteen or fifteen thousand pounds and 'never had any employment under the Crown, nor any private pecuniary reward from any Minister, though in general a friend to them'.[32] His disinterestedness appealed to that spirit of inde-

30. Richmond to Newcastle, Goodwood, 7 Jan. 1740/41: 32696, fols. 19–23.

31. Namier, *England in the Age of the American Revolution* (2d ed., New York, 1961), pp. 34–35 and n. 1.

32. Page to Newcastle, 22 Nov. 1758: 32885, fols. 507–08. Quoted in Namier, *Structure of Politics* (2d ed.), p. 126.

pendence which the Chichester electors cherished even while yielding to the magnetic attractions of Goodwood and Halland.

So important a person as John Page must, of course, be placated now that he could no longer be dished. Whereupon Newcastle turned to Archdeacon Ball. He asked him in January 1740/1 to do his best to remove in the minds of Page's friends and of Page's father-in-law, Alderman Soane, 'any ill impressions that may have been made to our prejudice', and Ball must tell Page and Soane—and Hutchins Williams—as well as any others he might think proper to approach, that Sir John Miller's intention of standing was neither in concert with himself nor with his knowledge. In this way Newcastle sidled up to prevarication. He thought it extremely hard, he continued, that Pelham and Butler should suffer in the opinion of Page's friends on account of Sir John's inclination. He then in confidence told Ball that had Sir John persisted in his plan, he would have had to support him on account of obligations to him for having so remarkably labored in support of Pelham and Butler, when Page by the circumstances of his interest could only at best observe a neutrality. Ball must read his letter to Dean Hargraves. This unlucky incident had given Newcastle great uneasiness: the thought of having zealous friends at Chichester anyways cooled toward his party was 'a great concern' to him. The Duke was 'very impatient' for Ball's report.[33]

As soon as he had received the Duke's commands Ball went his rounds. First, he called on the Alderman. He had the good fortune to find him alone and in the utmost good humor. 'After a long conference' Soane was satisfied that neither Newcastle nor Richmond had had any share in the 'supposed scheme' of setting up Sir John and 'that the word of two such honourable persons shall always weigh more with him than any insinuations from whatever quarter to the contrary'; Ball assured Newcastle that he might depend on the Alderman's

33. Newcastle to Ball, Newcastle House, 10 Jan. 1740/1: 32696, fol. 31.

vote and also upon his best interest in persuading his friends to favor the Duke's wishes.

Mr. Page had gone to the Quarter Sessions at Midhurst; he could not be visited. But Ball promised to see that Newcastle's obliging assurances would have their effect upon him and his friends. Should Page prove difficult, Ball would intimate that his continuing resentment must greatly abate the friendship and esteem that he himself had long shown him.

Mr. Hutchins Williams required more delicate handling, and so Ball hoped that the Duke would excuse him from waiting upon Williams until he had seen Page. Mr. Williams was a law to himself, 'a very silly purse proud fellow', said Richmond.[34] Ball agreed. A new man in Chichester, 'lay superior', as Disraeli might have observed, of Grey Friars, on the site of one of the city's two conventuals dissolved at the Reformation, Mr. Hutchins Williams knew himself to be a person of consequence. Both Richmond and Ball had already foreseen that he would probably not attend the meeting at Horsham in the summer of 1740 unless Newcastle honored him with a personal appeal. Ball advised a ducal letter. 'I verily think it would please his *wholeself* and pin the basket.'[35] It did, although not without some tetchiness in the personage at Grey Friars. Mr. Williams replied that notwithstanding it would be most inconvenient for him to be absent from home, yet upon his Grace's 'particular application' he was determined to be present at Horsham.[36]

Ball had an excellent reason for postponing his visit to Williams: 'next to Mrs. Williams, he's entirely (I had almost said implicitly) influenced' by Mr. Page. Without the latter's consent Ball had little hope of success at Grey Friars, although, were the new bishop, Dr. Matthias Mawson, 'under the known directions of your Grace, which his Lordship will own of course', to apply to Williams, his appeal must be 'peculiarly

34. Richmond to Newcastle, Goodwood, 30 July 1740: 32694, fol. 365.
35. Ball to Newcastle, Chichester, 28 July 1740: 32694, fol. 336.
36. Williams to Newcastle, Chichester, 1 Aug. 1740: 32694, fol. 389.

forcible as well as seasonable'. The Archdeacon concluded by saying that had he been permitted to read Newcastle's letter aloud to Williams, 'even where you declare in confidence what you must have done in case of a competition, I can't think but it must have had a great effect, impartially weighed, greater perhaps than anything I can offer under a less authentick direction'.[37]

Nine days later Ball sent Newcastle the news he had been so eagerly awaiting. Ball had seen Page; and Page, comforted by the express assurances of the two dukes, was now declaring himself 'very safe and well satisfied', and in addition to being ready to support Newcastle in county affairs was saying that 'the bulke of his natural and best friends' (including, we infer, Mr. Williams) was even now well inclined to Pelham and Butler.[38] As for Williams, Ball had heard that he was in perfect good humor again; a further proof, indeed, of Page's entire satisfaction over the removal of the 'design' to encourage Sir John. A little more work, and Williams in the spring of 1741 came round to supporting Lord Middlesex. One good turn deserved another. Since Williams had applied to Bishop Mawson on behalf of Page for the city of Chichester, Mawson offered to write to his 'old friend Mr. Hutchins Williams' and ask him to support Lord Middlesex for the county. The Bishop looked upon Mr. Williams as indebted to do him 'a good turn of this sort'.[39] Mawson's suggestion proved unnecessary. Ball, like the old mole, had worked in the ground so fast. On May 23 Williams notified Newcastle that, were Middlesex to stand, he considered him 'so unexceptionable a person in all respects, that I hope there will be no difficulty in supporting his pretensions'.[40] Williams, liking acidity, used negatives.

Archdeacon Ball had brilliantly executed his mission. He

37. Ball to Newcastle, Crocker Hill near Chichester, 14 Jan. 1740/1: 32696, fols. 38–39.
38. Ball to Newcastle, Chichester, 23 Jan. 1740/1: 32696, fol. 42.
39. Mawson to Newcastle, Cambridge, 24 May 1741: 32697, fol. 68.
40. Williams to Newcastle, Fryars, 23 May 1741: 32697, fol. 50.

had established his fitness to be dean. He was indeed, as New-castle told Richmond, 'the best agent we have in your parts'.[41]

Accordingly, during the second week of October 1741, Richmond wrote to Ball. The message informed him that he and Newcastle (the Duke allowed Richmond the doing of the favor) would like, should Hargraves die, to see him dean. On October 13 Ball replied—and ambiguously declined the deanery of Chichester.

The occasion was most secret, highly piquant, and stirring enough to startle Ball into writing his most characteristic prose. His intimacy with the Duke of Richmond was now well established and confident, the regard mutual. How rewarding for Ball to see his services acknowledged; to picture the familiar ritual of a dean's installation in the cathedral; to re-ceive the congratulations of the Bishop, of Backshell, Clarke, and the prebendaries; to behold the confusion of Canon Parke! Into his reply Ball put all that part of himself with which Richmond was well acquainted. He wrote his master-piece.

'Your Grace's most obliging message,' he began, 'came too late and was of too much moment to admit of a full answer by the last post.' Since Hargraves seemed not to be in any immediate danger of death, Ball hoped that Richmond would 'the more easily excuse this short delay' in his acknowledg-ment. He was, of course, infinitely obliged to the Duke of Richmond and his other great friends for the high honor and favor first designed him in the event of a vacancy. Then, turn-ing halfway from the shock of a blunt refusal, he expressed himself conditionally. He would not decline any station

> in which I could be further serviceable to your interest, however unworthy I might think myself of it in other respects and however inconsiderable it might appear to

41. Newcastle to Richmond, Whitehall, 20 Sept. 1740: Goodwood MSS, Box 25. For Richmond's even more enthusiastic opinion of Ball, see his letter to Newcastle, Goodwood, 19 Sept. 1746: 32708, fol. 338.

me in point of personal advantage. But I can't see, my Lord Duke, how it could possibly answer your ends or my own unless I could keep my archdeaconry and some other little things I now enjoy along with the deanery.

Ball proceeded to catalogue his objections. As Archdeacon of Chichester and judge of the ecclesiastical court he had a pretty considerable intercourse with and influence over members of the clergy, church wardens, and other freeholders in western Sussex; whereas the authority and interest of a dean of Chichester, being infinitely less extensive, was chiefly confined to the city and suburbs. (Lord Esher, we remember, declined the viceroyalty of India on the grounds that it would make his influence parochial.) Even within the city a dean had no greater capacity of 'doing good offices or engaging more persons to his interest than an active and hospitable residentiary with the same spirit and fortune'. The dean, moreover, had just the same share as a canon in the disposal of places belonging to the cathedral and, so Ball had often remarked, was apter to make enemies than friends when compelled to punish delinquents and maintain discipline in the choir.

Such were Ball's more general objections to taking the deanery. He came now to personal reasons. Were he to exchange his archdeaconry for the deanery, his income would in all probability not advance above £10 a year certain;

> for which I must be 250 or 300 £ out of pocket presently, leave, what I think, a more convenient house to my brother *Parke,* after haveing just expended above 400 £ upon it and be obliged to live in a less eligible because in a more envyed and shewey situation. If indeed I were allowed to keep everything I now have except my Residentiaryship along with the Deanery it might doubtless give an additional influence in favour of my great friends and the common cause and I might be made whole agen in about two years time; but this I only mention to shew your Grace (and if you please any other great friends

73

through your hands) how the case would really stand on the most advantageous supposition, having no particular inclination at all to the Deanery on any terms, much less on such as might appear engrossing or unprecedented, so that if, as I don't in the least doubt, my superiours can as effectually answer their own and the publick purposes any other way and oblige us with an able and good Whig Governour it will be full as agreeable to me.

Ball bowed low in gratitude and ventured to hope for 'the future assistence of such good friends in any other reasonable addition I might hereafter desire to the great happiness I already enjoy through their good offices and intercession'. Discreetly he refrained for the moment from suggesting some lesser though specific reward for his ambiguous self-denial.

Thomas Ball would not have been himself had he not at the last moment yielded to impulse. He began to wheedle and to pour his distillment into the porches of his patron's ear. He would submit to Richmond's superior judgment and direction; he was in no sense moved by selfishness or the wish to save expense but solely by a view to the interest of Goodwood; he would always, he said again, accept of any station of the most disadvantageous sort, should Richmond expect it of him, 'as most for your own and the publick service'.

Ball closed with an admonition. 'If (as I secretly wish on your accounts as well as our own) another of our body, who is at present unprovided with a house, should be pitched upon to succeed poor Dean Hargraves', he wished to be told promptly. In sum, were William Clarke, as Ball correctly surmised, under consideration for the deanery, there would result a vacancy among the residentiaries. If such should happen, Newcastle would then be 'much pestered' by Mr. Hutchins Williams and perhaps some others to bestow the place on their own candidate. Their man was George Adams, vicar of two little parishes near Arundel and Prebendary of Wittering, 'a creature of Williams', Ball added, who would as a residentiary

74

both from his attachment 'at least, and out of principle too do all possible prejudice to the general interest and your Grace's especially at Chichester'. Besides, John Parke, 'if not my brother Backshell' (John Backshell had recently by a second marriage become Ball's brother-in-law[42]) was 'well disposed to him already'. Ball now pricked Richmond with the traditional alarm over capitular influence: were George Adams to be admitted residentiary, 'there would soon be an entire end of the Whigg chapter and the publick interest'. For what in that event could Ball do? How could Ball and 'honest' William Clarke breast the waves of Opposition when agitated by Parke and Adams with the assistance of wobbling Backshell? On the supposition that the two dukes might now prefer to invite Canon Clarke to succeed Dean Hargraves, Ball confessed that he had 'no particular and proper prebendary to propose', not even Walter Barttelot. He apologized for meddling in a matter 'so much out of my sphere' and smoothly ended his extraordinary epistle by hoping for the dukes' sake 'as well as ours' that care would be taken 'to preserve an indisputable majority of true Whiggs in the Chapter of Chichester. I am, my Lord Duke, with the utmost esteem and gratitude . . .'[43]

Ball stepped wide of an absolute refusal. He begged to be allowed to have his cake and eat it too. Characteristically he made his acceptance conditional: he would take the deanery if he could keep his archdeaconry besides those trifles he already possessed. If not, then perhaps Canon Clarke would become dean. But that way, he pointed out, danger lurked.

How had Ball learned that his patrons were also considering Canon Clarke for the deanery? We do not know. Let it suffice that Richmond, a week before he received Ball's reply, gave

42. *Calendar of Sussex Marriage Licenses*, Sussex Record Society, 32 (1926), p. 61. Hargraves to ———, Chichester, 7 March 1740/1: 32696, fol. 200.

43. Ball to Richmond, Chichester, 13 Oct. 1741: 32698, fols. 132–33. For the complete text of Ball's letter see Appendix below.

Newcastle his present view: 'If the archdeacon were not in the way, I do assure you that I should like Mr. Clarke preferably to anybody, firstly because he belongs to you, and secondly because wee could not have a better man'.[44]

In one respect Richmond was partly mistaken, in another quite right. William Clarke would never have agreed that he 'belonged' to Newcastle. And there can be no doubt that he would have made an exemplary, if somewhat novel, dean of Chichester. He was before all things a Christian pastor. So much and more William Hayley said of him, however much he relished Ball's gaiety and benevolence of heart. The two canons had one accomplishment in common: both wrote English verse with elegance and ease. In essentials they could not have been more unlike: Ball in his preferments served the State and the social conventions which made eigh'teenth-century England stolid; Clarke preferred the interests of the Church, and so admirably managed the jarring passions of the Chapter's members that it was said after his death, 'the peace of the church of Chichester has expired with Mr. Clarke'.[45] He would have made a good dean. His learning was sound and urbane. He knew as much about Mr. Pope as he did about his Romans and Saxons. He never tired, in spite of a moderate income, of bestowing charity—'it was his custom,' Hayley wrote, 'to devote a shilling in every guinea that he received, to the service of the poor . . . He was a man of unaffected piety, and evangelical singleness of heart.'[46]

Hayley did not exaggerate. Clarke asked for nothing. He was content with his family, his books and scholarship, his indolence, his friends, his love of open sea or Downs, and his all-saving joy in watching the antics of his fellow men. Originally from Shropshire, he had known Parke when the two were fellows of St. John's, Cambridge. His academic distinctions brought him while very young a chaplaincy to a bishop.

44. Richmond to Newcastle, Wilton, 5 Oct. 1741: 32698, fol. 102.
45. Nichols, *Literary Anecdotes, 4,* 368.
46. Ibid., p. 374.

Soon he occupied the office of domestic chaplain in the train of his lifelong friend, the Duke of Newcastle. At the recommendation of his father-in-law and without any solicitation of his own, Archbishop Wake presented him to an archiepiscopal peculiar in Sussex, the rectory of Buxted *cum* Uckfield in 1724.[47] What with the hop gardens it was worth at least £300 a year and afforded the incumbent an excellent house, gardens, stables, and fishponds.[48] Three years later he became a prebendary of Chichester, and in 1738/39 Newcastle secured his admission into the Chapter (a plan that the Duke had had in mind since at least 1735) in succession to Gooch. In return for these favors Clarke's superiors appear to have expected political services. Clarke did indeed exert himself in the election of 1734 and reported that 'Buxted would be an entire parish' for the Whigs. Yet he could not take himself seriously in the role of political agent. When Wake upon presenting him to Buxted expressed the hope that 'he might make the duke of Newcastle his friend by voting for him as occasion should serve', Clarke replied, 'Ay, sure'.[49]

He had, moreover, a sense of the balance of things, of the necessity to keep proportion in the acts of living. He did not run to excess. He was no snuffling oddity solely occupied with the study of old coins. His letters to the London printer, William Bowyer, contain as many recondite references as does the correspondence of other eighteenth-century antiquaries. They are also filled with sunlight. He beguiles his friends with the pleasantness of Brighton:

> such a tract of sea, such regions of corn . . . we have little conversation beside the *clamor nauticus*, which is here a sort of treble to the plashing of the waves against the cliffe. My morning business is, bathing in the sea, and

47. *S.A.C.*, 26 (1875), 21.
48. Robert Wake to Abp. Wake, 12 July 1720: Arch. W. Epist. 21, item ccxlvii, 353, quoted by Sykes, *Church and State*, p. 213.
49. Sykes, *Church and State*, p. 83.

then buying fish; the evening is, riding out for air, view-
ing the old Saxon camps, and counting the ships in the
road . . . Do come and join us here . . . we do just what
we like; we are bound by no conventionalities.[50]

He rises from his papers and capitular 'trifles', from Gothofred,
Greaves, or Scipio Maffei's works, to enjoy the open air. 'A
ride or two on the side of our hills are better than five pages
in Seneca and Sir Roger L'Estrange.'[51] He might seek balance
in life; he could not bring himself to conform.

Herein lay his difference from Ball. Clarke was bland, Ball
obsequious. Clarke saw through and around the assumptions
of a society dominated by landed proprietors; his humor
blended with his sense of fitness to keep him detached and
constantly amused. The Archdeacon, for all his scheming,
never questioned why the hierarchy of powers in Sussex func-
tioned as it did. Clarke was ever laughing—a Yorick of Sussex.
Il 'se fout de nous', Richmond told Newcastle, 'and says he
shall never ask any favour from you or me. He is a sad dog'.[52]
'We country parsons,' Clarke mused, 'have some resemblance
with the parish bells—never speak, unless three or four country fellows tug hard at us, and then it is only to give notice
that somebody is married, or dead.'[53] 'A meek quiet thing',
he wrote about himself, 'not vain enough to desire to be
thought a scholar'; he set himself up 'for still-life, and should
succeed tolerably well, if it was not for a set of country squires,
who are as troublesome here as authors are in town, and not
quite so profitable'.[54] When he saw 'our gentlemen' recon-
noitering the county against the next election, he smiled: 'We
toil much about trifles; puffing interest, as booksellers do

50. Clarke to Bowyer, Brighthelmstone, 22 July 1736: William Bowyer,
Miscellaneous Tracts (London, 1785), p. 554. *S.A.C., 19* (1867), 165–66.
    51. Clarke to Bowyer, 15 March 1757: Bowyer, p. 586.
    52. Richmond to Newcastle, Goodwood, 8 Sept. 1738: 32691, fol. 344.
    53. Clarke to Bowyer, 17 Sept. 1737: Bowyer, p. 557.
    54. Ibid., 1738, 1743, and n.d: Bowyer, pp. 558, 579, 583.

authors, and perhaps to as little purpose.'[55] Richmond died in 1750. Shortly before his death the Dean and Chapter granted him permission to construct a vault under the Lady Chapel for his family. His remains were duly placed there, and an inscription upon the vault ended with the sentence, *Hæc est Domus ultima.* Clarke's sense of absurdity blossomed into verse:

> Did he, who thus inscrib'd the wall,
> Not read, or not believe St. Paul,
> Who says there is, where'er it stands,
> Another house not made with hands,
> Or may we gather from these words,
> That house is not a house of Lords?[56]

In 1737 Clarke got the fright of his life. 'I was for a few days,' he wrote, 'in great fear of an archdeaconry; but was very happily delivered from that dignity. Next to the hazards of the press, the most terrible thing is a small dignity in the church.'[57]

No, Richmond and probably Newcastle to the contrary, Mr. Clarke would never do for dean.

At Grey Friars, Hutchins Williams sketched his grand design. He, too, had a protégé among the cathedral prebendaries. He would do something for George Adams. In his letter of October 24 he led forth from rumor. Were one of the residentiaries, as was reported, to become dean in the event of

55. Clarke to Bowyer, ?1733: Bowyer, p. 573.

56. Nichols, *Literary Anecdotes, 4,* 372–73. Francis W. Steer, 'The Funeral Account of the First Duke of Richmond and Lennox', *S.A.C., 98* (1960), 163–64.

57. Clarke to Bowyer, 7 Feb. 1736/7 or 1737/8: Bowyer, p. 556. On 8 April 1767 Clarke wrote to Bowyer: 'I could tell you a secret, which nobody knows but my wife; that if our Deanry should be ever vacant in my time (which is not likely) I would not accept it . . . I have learnt to know that at the end of life these things are not worth our notice.' Nichols, *Literary Anecdotes, 4,* 369–70.

Hargraves' death, would the Duke promote Adams to the vacancy? 'There is no doubt,' he cajoled, 'but the Chapter will always be determined by your Grace, in their choice of a residentiary.' Adams, besides having 'an exceeding good character as a clergyman, has a great ambition to serve your Grace'.[58] Newcastle had doubtless received Ball's warning from Richmond. On October 29 he replied: the expected demise of the dean might not open a vacancy among the residentiaries; with ducal regrets he confessed himself not to be at liberty to do what Mr. Adams now desired.[59]

The dukes had a third string to their bow—no less a person than the Rev. William Ashburnham, the very semblance of that 'able and good Whig Governour' whom Ball had advised. Ashburnham, it must be admitted, had got ahead, and in one instance by being ungenerous. Back in 1717 Archbishop Wake had greatly befriended a young Swiss, John Henry Ott, son of the Archdeacon of Zurich. Wake placed him in the library at Lambeth, ordained him himself, made him his chaplain, and showered preferments upon him, notably, in 1723, the goodly living of Bexhill on the Sussex coast midway between Eastbourne and Hastings.[60] In 1737 Wake died, leaving his foreign-born protégé wedged into the diocese of Chichester and subject to Pelhamite convenience. Ashburnham, who was at the time rector of both Cromwell and Gamston in Nottinghamshire, wished, it would seem, for a benefice nearer his family in Sussex. He coveted Bexhill, possibly for political reasons. He turned to Newcastle to aid him. Together they eased Ott out of Bexhill by persuading him that if he exchanged that living for Ashburnham's two rectories in Nottinghamshire, they could promise him the equivalent value. Ott consented in order to oblige Ashburnham. Two years later, in 1741, he was nearing despair. Bexhill he now found

58. Williams to Newcastle, Fryars, 24 Oct. 1741: 32698, fols. 216–17.

59. Newcastle to Williams, Newcastle House, 29 Oct. 1741: 32698, fol. 231.

60. Sykes, *William Wake*, 2, 17–18.

80

to be worth at least double what he had in lieu of it, the loss had not been made up, and he had many children to support. He besought Newcastle either to procure him an equivalent living or to dispose Ashburnham to let him return to Bexhill.[61] Ashburnham held on to Bexhill, and Ott had to hold on to Cromwell and Gamston. The 'disadvantage' was 'thought to have hastened his end'.[62]

Ashburnham was now thirty-one. He possessed assets. He had 'a voice and elocution peculiarly suited to sacred language'.[63] He was both a royal chaplain and a chaplain of the Royal Hospital at Chelsea. And more, he was very well connected. He stood to succeed to Broomham, the estate of his uncle, Sir William Ashburnham, Bt., in the parish of Guestling near Hastings. Upon his father's death he would also inherit the baronetcy. His family was prominent in Sussex and claimed distant kinship with yet another of Newcastle's natural allies, the young Earl of Ashburnham of Ashburnham Place; his uncle, Sir William Ashburnham, had in turn represented Hastings and Seaford almost continuously from 1710 to the last election; in 1733 he knew he could throw at least three hundred freeholders' votes to the support of Pelham and Butler.[64] Of equal if not greater moment in young William Ashburnham's career were his family's alliances with the Pelhams. Uncle William had married Margaret Pelham, a cousin of the Duke's. William followed suit and in 1736 married her niece, who was a sister of Thomas Pelham, Newcastle's present member for Lewes. Besides, young William was, like Newcastle, a Cambridge man. As vicar of Bexhill, he was known to the lord of the manor, the Duke of Dorset, as well as to the patron of the living, the Bishop of Chichester. In fact, it was

61. Ott to Newcastle, Gamston, 18 Feb. 1740/1: 32696, fol. 103; 4 July 1741: 32697, fols. 278–79.

62. Nichols, *Literary Anecdotes, 9*, 322. *S.A.C., 53* (1910), 107.

63. Hayley, *Memoirs, 1*, 98.

64. Henry Pelham to Newcastle, Broomham, 18 Sept. 1733: 32688, fols. 345–46.

Bishop Mawson who took the trouble of telling William that the Dean was 'in a very declining way'. William's aunt, Margaret Pelham, took up his cause. She wrote to Newcastle. She mentioned the Bishop's letter to her nephew about Hargraves' illness and the deanery. 'I can't think,' she said, 'he cou'd mention it to him for any other reason than to put him upon making early application to your Grace that he may succeed him in the deanery of Chichester.'[65] What a felicitous proposal! Here in Ashburnham was the clerical counterpart of Lord Middlesex. Make him dean! At one stroke his appointment would give Chichester a dean of social prominence, lock and seal the Ashburnham interest on behalf of Lord Middlesex in the approaching by-election, and pleasure the Duke of Newcastle by opening to him yet another opportunity of packing a relative into public office.

65. M. Ashburnham to Newcastle, Broomham, 10 Oct. 1741: 32698, fol. 118.

FOUR. THE OUTCOME

AND SO while the decision was being taken in the utmost secrecy and, apparently, with Bishop Mawson acting as intermediary between the dukes and the Ashburnhams, November brought the drama to its culmination. Dean Hargraves was given over; 'he is very bad', Richmond informed Newcastle on the sixth.[1] Mrs. Hargraves sent for her fifteen-year-old son Thomas from Westminster School. Rumors flew across the county. Tensions mounted. The now certain elevation of the Dean to Heaven and of some presbyter to the deanery of Chichester disclosed a horizon of bright promotions. A move, indeed several moves, were about to occur in the unending game of preferment. Who would get what? The social structure of Sussex was on the verge of a convulsion. Nothing would ever again be quite what it had been.

Meanwhile Sergison, if he had actually gone into Somersetshire, had returned to Cuckfield. During the last days of September they gave him an entertainment at Mayfield. Six footmen dressed in white and some eight women bearing a garland quaintly advanced to meet the candidate and his friends. Twelve small earthen guns prepared by a potter of Wadhurst fired the salute. The women danced before the Royal Oak. The candidate and his party then withdrew to receive their voting friends, who numbered around thirty. The evening closed with half a hogshead of strong beer set out for the populace, the six men in white drinking success to Mr. Sergison amid the ringing of bells and loud huzzas, and the candidate distributing guineas to his entertainers.[2] In October he tried

1. Richmond to Newcastle, 6 Nov. 1741: 32698, fol. 268.
2. Rev. Richard Downall to ——— Atkins, Mayfield, 30 Sept. 1741: 32698, fol. 83.

something rather more ambitious. He extended invitations to a treat to no less than ten neighboring parishes: 'there did not go fifty freeholders to him', John Board told Newcastle, whereupon Sergison was 'very much in the dumps'. He next made a cricket match for forty guineas to be played in his own park. By crying it at all the neighboring parishes he drew a great concourse of people to his doors. One of Newcastle's agents, guessing his intention of soliciting votes, sent spies 'to keep a strict watch on the motions of the enemy, and to use their utmost art and diligence in the service of Lord Middlesex'. Sergison, as usual, astonished his guests. He canvassed not at all nor did he ask the players, who won his money, either to eat or drink with him, much to their disappointment and chagrin.[3]

Then, shortly before November 6, Richmond held an important conference with Archdeacon Ball. He opened to him the scheme of naming Ashburnham to succeed Hargraves. Ball expressed himself as 'perfectly well satisfied and pleased . . . butt' (did Richmond catch the abrupt, so familiar conjunction?) 'he says that as the Chancellor is butt a little older than himself he shall have butt a very distant prospect of that, so he shou'd be glad to have a promis of the Bishop for the liveing of Selsea, or the Chancellorship, whichsoever should first become vacant, not both'.[4] The Archdeacon had at length launched his own campaign for a reward.

Matters now again became oppressively complicated. Ball was fetching up a new, somewhat astonishing request and one, moreover, that in the granting would require much delicacy of address. And here, too, was Canon Richard Green, another of Richmond's ducklings and his chaplain, a graduate of Cambridge, and rector of both Marston and Birdham, who deserved to move to a better seat among the musical chairs. Back in early October, Richmond had asked Newcastle to let

3. John Board to Newcastle, Paxhill, 29 Oct. 1741: 32698, fols. 229–30.
4. Richmond to Newcastle, Goodwood, 6 Nov. 1741: 32698, fols. 268–69.

84

Green succeed to Ball's residentiaryship, should Ball become Dean. "There can be no objection to him,' he urged, 'butt his *small talke*. There can be none against his actions; for he is incapable of doing a bad thing, and I assure you his talke is mended, nay, he's grown quite good.'[5] Since the selection of Ashburnham precluded a vacancy in the Chapter, all that Green now wanted was Ashburnham's chaplaincy of Chelsea Hospital—'the thing upon earth that he has all his life wished most for'. Newcastle replied that he would do his best. In the event he made Richmond appear ridiculous. Newcastle had recently met Richmond at the Duke of St. Albans'; he had then told Richmond to write to Henry Pelham and thank him for preferring Green to the chaplaincy; Newcastle had assured Richmond that Green's advancement was his brother Henry's own thought and proposal. Newcastle now forgot what he had said. He wrote Richmond to say that the latter should write to Pelham 'to *make a strong application* to him' for Chelsea. But how could Richmond do that? He had already thanked Pelham. 'So,' Richmond thought, 'an application after thanks would be somewhat awkward. However if you thinke it's propper, I will do it with great pleasure, and I at first thought as I told you that it was decent to begin that way.'[6] It was all most confusing.

Dean Hargraves died on the morning of November 16. Ball was quick to inform Richmond. The poor Dean, he said, had the satisfaction to see and know his son. Ball's next sentence betrayed his own feelings. 'I intend to acquaint his Grace the Duke of Newcastle with this melancholy news by tomorrow's post but trust entirely to your Grace's good offices with him, Mr. Pelham, and the bishop in relation to the promise of Selsey living or the chancellorship, which shall first happen, not doubting but such an alternative will be thought reasonable enough . . .' Ball now pressed his case with

5. Richmond to Newcastle, Goodwood, 2 Oct. 1741: 32698, fol. 94.
6. Ibid., 11 Nov. 1741: 32698, fol. 306.

ardor: his meriting the promise for having given up all pretensions to a station so much desired by the Bishop and by Mr. Ashburnham; his securing the reversion of either of the preferments ('as to the chancellorship at least, I hope, very distant') would be more agreeable to him than 'a more exalted situation in the church'; his hopes of convincing his great and good friends of being thereby enabled to serve them and 'the good old Cause'.[7] Next day Ball addressed himself to Newcastle. In almost the same words that he had used in his letter to Richmond he recounted the last moments of the Dean. Exercising unaccustomed restraint, he chose not to trouble Newcastle with any of his own 'favourite requests . . . on this mournfull occasion'. He sent him his heartiest wishes for a worthy successor, about whom he confessed himself to be 'in no pain . . . as long as this and every station in our Church are so justly under your Grace's auspicious influence and direction'.[8] Was Ball also trying, as he might have said, to pin the basket?

The two preferments on which Ball had cast a sanguine eye were in the Bishop's gift. The chancellorship, which Ball had for years been regarding as 'a most desireable piece of preferment and what the two preceding bishops were pleased to think I had peculiar pretensions to', had been held ever since 1719 by the Rev. Prebendary Robert Rawlinson, a priest much distressed by reason of having some thirteen children, descendants of old Bishop Bowers, who had died before he could do much for his son-in-law.[9] The parish of Selsey lay seven miles from Chichester, its rectory perhaps the most lucrative benefice in the environs of the city.[10] This living was at present held by a clergyman whose career, like that of his brother,

7. Ball to Richmond, Chichester, 16 Nov. 1741: 32698, fol. 323.
8. Ball to Newcastle, Chichester, 17 Nov. 1741: 32698, fol. 334.
9. Francis Hare to Newcastle, 12 May 1737: 32690, fol. 285.
10. In 1797 the rectory of Selsey was reported to be worth near £400. G. L. Gomme, ed., *The Gentleman's Magazine Library*, *24* (1900), *English Topography*, Pt. xii, 314; both Dallaway (*Western Sussex*, *1*, Pt. ii, 9)

succinctly illustrates the forces of influence and patronage extending throughout the diocese in the eighteenth century. Thomas and Simon Manningham were the sons of Thomas Manningham, Bishop of Chichester from 1709 to 1722. During his father's episcopate Thomas picked up the treasurership and a prebend of Chichester, a prebend of Westminster, and the rectories of both Slinfold and Selsey in Sussex. He kept these preferments until death shook him loose in 1750 and started a fresh redistribution.[11]

Both Chancellor Rawlinson and Thomas Manningham were in 1741 about sixty years of age. Ball, now forty-three, had therefore reason to be hopeful of succeeding one or the other fairly soon. But the prospect offered embarrassments. The more Richmond pressed Newcastle to press the Bishop for a promise of the reversion of whichever preferment should fall first, the more uncomfortable Ball became. Richmond knew how to be insistent: Ball's request was 'really very reasonable', he wrote to Newcastle, 'I need not tell you that he is a fast friend, a man of great weight in this part of the country, to be absolutely depended upon, and of an unexceptionable character'.[12] The thing was so reasonable in itself. And so very imminent? Ball winced at the indelicacy of his request. He could not, he admitted, bring himself to think of a vacancy in Rawlinson's chancellery with either 'pleasure or even patience', and so he hoped that Newcastle would 'be able to indulge him with another, less unpleasing and perhaps a nearer view, vizt: of Selsey living'. Why less unpleasing? Why nearer? Was Manningham hopelessly infirm? Or influenced perhaps by the 'Tory' lord of the manor of Selsey, Sir John

---

and Horsfield (*Sussex*, 2, 36) mention the considerable value of the living. Cf. Edward Heron-Allen, *Selsey Bill, Historic and Pre-Historic* (London, 1911), pp. 219–20.

11. His brother Simon was almost as happily beneficed—a prebend of Chichester in addition to two livings within the diocese.

12. Richmond to Newcastle, Goodwood, 18 Nov. 1741: 32698, fol. 338.

Peachey?[13] Might not Ball's presence in the parish, where in 1734 a majority of freeholders had voted for Bisshopp,[14] bring these stray sheep back into the Whig fold and undermine Parke's influence in the region? Ball's yearning for Selsey underscored his noted benevolence. Could he succeed to Selsey, he would, he told Newcastle, resign his vicarage of Eartham in favor of 'an honest and ingenious and poor nephew now upon my hands'. He wished Bishop Mawson to know that his motive proceeded 'from a compassionate and not a covetous principle and especially as his lordship will have a good prebend and another good living to give away' in the event of Dr. Manningham's death.[15] Did Thomas Ball now begin to suspect that Bishop Mawson also had a scheme for the disposal of the chancellorship or the living of Selsey?

Meanwhile, sorrow and commotion filled the deanery. Hargraves was duly buried in the cathedral and, according to his desire, by the side of his old friend and Newcastle's protégé, Bishop Bowers.[16] His widow now showed her mettle. She had her young son write to Newcastle on the day after his father's death. The boy, commendably mingling grief for his 'papa' with gratitude to his family's patron, advised the Duke that since he was unable to return to Westminster, his 'mama' intended to send him to Canon Clarke's at Christmas. He asked Newcastle's leave to go. 'Your Grace knows very well that I shall lose no study while I am with him.'[17] Within a week Mrs. Hargraves was putting off her servants and arranging to send Thomas to Mr. Clarke. She herself was about to leave the lonely deanery for Archdeacon Ball's own hospitable, even hilarious, home next door. There she intended to stay until

13. Heron-Allen, *Selsey Bill,* pp.180–81.
14. Ibid., p. 265.
15. Ball to Newcastle, Chichester, 24 Nov. 1741: 32698, fols. 373–74.
16. Ibid., fol. 373.
17. Thomas Hargraves to Newcastle, Chichester, 17 Nov. 1741: 32698, fol. 332.

she could settle her affairs with her late husband's successor and see what he might want of her goods and furniture.[18]

It was for the widow and the orphan to mourn. For others the Dean's death excited clamorous appeals from persons who wished to be remembered in the division of the spoils. The Ashburnhams and their friends exulted. Newcastle, in a year when he received over thirty-two applications for ecclesiastical appointments,[19] found himself afflicted by a spate of askings issuing from the death of the Dean of Chichester.

The earliest was once more the Rev. Walter Barttelot's. Mr. Barttelot had just learned of the Dean's death. He would not now presume to trouble His Grace with a repetition of his request that Newcastle recommend him to the King to succeed Dr. Hargraves. He wrote only to remind the Duke of his having been enabled through Newcastle's goodness to serve His Majesty as military chaplain for more than sixteen years. He hoped that this appointment would carry as much weight as if he had had the honor of being one of the King's domestic chaplains.[20]

A week after Hargraves died there came from Thomas Archer, the member for Bramber, a plea to befriend the Rev. Rice Williams. Archer was possibly the reason why the shabby contests between two rival families for control of that borough ceased after 1734, not to revive until the election of 1768. There being at Bramber thirty-six burgage houses,[21] the tenants of which, paying scot and lot, enjoyed the right of election, control of these dwellings had off and on for a century harassed the two factions and at Westminster consumed the time of members in hearing petitions and passing resolutions. Archer had had by 1761 the last three returns there for

18. Ball to Newcastle, Chichester, 24 Nov. 1741: 32698, fol. 373.

19. Perkins, 'Electioneering in the Eighteenth Century', p. 110.

20. Barttelot to Newcastle, Duke Street at the corner of Germain Street, Piccadilly, 19 Nov. 1741: 32698, fol. 343.

21. W. D. Cooper, in Horsfield, *Sussex*, 2, App., 33.

his friends. Should anyone try to surprise him at Bramber (the inhabitants were very poor), he had only to pull down the houses to make the borough 'absolutely his own'.[22] He was a faithful adherent of Newcastle's and Walpole's. He merited a favor. He much hoped the report was true that Prebendary Wilson of Worcester Cathedral was to succeed Hargraves. If so, he and his brother, member for Warwick, would welcome the Duke's securing from the Crown the stall at Worcester for the Rev. Rice Williams, one of the King's chaplains. The two brothers had Williams' promotion much at heart, and since the lives of the prebendaries of Worcester happened to be in general 'very good', the Archers had long awaited some such God-given opportunity of serving him. Newcastle's kindness, Archer concluded, would lay his brother and himself under the greatest obligations.[23] Behind the politeness one glimpses two steady votes for the Duke in the House of Commons.

Newcastle heard also from an old acquaintance in Kent. The Rev. Thomas Curteis, rector of Wrotham, and of Sevenoaks, where lay Knole, the Duke of Dorset's vast Tudor mansion, was someone whom Newcastle could neither in tenderness nor in self-interest ignore. Mr. Curteis, in the first place, had influence: his relations populated Tenterden in Kent, and some of them were Sussex freeholders whom in 1733 he had hoped to persuade to vote as Newcastle wished; he had Dorset's ear; and his son Thomas waited not only upon Dorset's spiritual needs as His Grace's domestic chaplain but also upon his political. In the election of 1734 young Thomas, braving violence, had been most industrious in abetting Dorset's cause both in Kent and in the corporation of Hythe, one of the Cinque Ports, of which Dorset was Lord Warden. Solely to serve Newcastle's interest Curteis had made his son a freeholder in Sussex and had himself done his best

22. *Report on State of Elections, Sussex* [1762]: Henry E. Huntington Library and Art Gallery, Stowe MSS, 18th Century, uncatalogued.
23. Archer to Newcastle, 23 Nov. 1741: 32698, fol. 361.

to defend Lord Middlesex's desperate campaign for the county of Kent by writing a twenty-page pamphlet in support of the ministers.[24] Curteis and his son, unlike Archdeacon Ball, respected the decencies: young Thomas had indeed fixed his eye upon Hargraves' rectory of Waldron, but neither father nor son had thought it 'honourable, or decent' to apply for it before the incumbent was dead. Now, in 1741, old Thomas was tired, indeed exhausted by his seventy-five years and attended with constant rheumatic pains; he had several daughters to provide for; and he so much hoped that Newcastle would remember Thomas—'no person bears a better character as a clergyman with the gentry and all others that know him'; 'a good character, for learning, sobriety, and a true knowledge of the world'.[25] He asked for Thomas, not for himself. They were distressed, he said, that Newcastle had put aside Thomas' just and reasonable views about Waldron and secured the rectory for another person. Thomas, as things went, was already sufficiently pressed by the circumstances of children and the need to support 'with decency, his station and character'. So if Thomas could not have Waldron, he would be infinitely indebted to Newcastle if he could have the prebend of Westminster left vacant by the death of Dean Hargraves.

Robert Austen was obliged to ask for the pickings. Prebendaries, domestic chaplains, and otherwise beneficed clergy might count on their interest in order to fall heirs to something of Hargraves'—his deanery, his stall in Westminster Abbey, or his rectories of East Hoathly and Waldron. Such men expected to be favored: they had served either Newcastle or the King or they relied upon their immediate patrons to lift up imploring voices on their behalf to the Duke. Robert Austen had nothing, beyond the arguments of debts and need, to justify his timorous request. He was merely one among that horde of stipendiary curates who scraped along on the charity

24. Curteis to Newcastle, Wrotham, 3, 15 Sept. 1733: 32688, fols. 246, 336; 19 Nov. 1733: 33344, fols. 69–90.

25. Ibid., 21 June 1740: 32693, fol. 406; 24 Nov. 1741: 32698, fol. 371.

of their clerical employers, curates like Thomas Brockbank,[26] Sterne's James Kilner,[27] and Robert Robson, who for a quarter of a century (1753–78) served as curate of Cocking and Selham in western Sussex without preferment.[28] Austen had possibly one flashing recollection: he had known Sterne at Jesus, where together the two undergraduates, fated to be so different in point of fame and station, had been sizars. In 1733 Austen had been ordained deacon and licensed to perform the office of curate in the parish of Burwash, where he lived.[29] His difficulties may be surmised from his need to pay for his education and the support of his mother as well as from his failure to be ordained priest until 1736[30] and his inability to proceed to his degree at Cambridge until two years later. In the summer of 1739 he had duly waited upon the Duke and received from him those kind assurances of favoring him whenever anything proper should fall vacant, assurances that the Duke so readily gave to the insignificant. Next year in the hope that Newcastle would pity him and help him, he asked for the living of Westfield.[31] He did not get it. His stipend was only £40, and he was gradually slipping into the ways of clerical mendicants. Surely, he thought, among the several avoidances resulting from Hargraves' death there might be something for him. 'If the death of the Dean of Chichester,' he wrote on November 24, 1741, to Ashburnham's brother-in-law, Colonel James Pelham, 'shall cause any vacancy which I may be thought proper to supply, I humbly

26. *Diary and Letter Book of Thomas Brockbank, 1671–1709*, ed. R. Trappes-Lomax (Manchester, Chetham Society, 1930).

27. *Letters of Laurence Sterne*, ed. L. P. Curtis (Oxford, Clarendon Press, 1935, 1965), *s.v.* Kilner, James.

28. Sykes, *Church and State*, pp. 203–05. George Smith and Frank Benger, *The Oldest London Bookshop* (London, 1928).

29. West Sussex County Record Office, *Subscription Book, 1724–54*, p. 108.

30. Ibid., p. 134.

31. Austen to ——, Salehurst, 4 July 1740: 32693, fol. 452.

entreat your favour and assistance in the affair . . . If I am too pressing in any application (which I would willingly avoid), I hope you will impute it to my occasions.'[32]

By November 24, the day on which Austen wrote to Colonel Pelham, the secret of Ashburnham's appointment to the deanery had become public. Archdeacon Ball sent his congratulations to Newcastle along with his request for the reversions. He took the occasion to be spiteful. He could not imagine, he wrote, that the intended advancement of William Ashburnham would be disagreeable to any member of the Chapter,

> not even to our president Mr. Parke himself, who on the score of old family intimacies will, I dare say, be as civil and respectful to our new dean as he can possibly bring himself to be to any of our true friends, who of course will often have occasion to be upon their guard and even to thwart him in his ever intriguing, political capacity when in Chichester.

Of course Ashburnham could count on Ball's aid. Ball was himself all readiness to concur with him in any measure that might 'promote the Whig interest in general and that of your Grace, the great Sussex-Supporter of it, in particular'.[33] Richmond too rejoiced and with none of Ball's acerbity. He hoped they would have 'our new dean' soon, he assured Newcastle. 'I never revealed this secret nor any other, butt every body either knew it, or guessed it here; and seem mightily pleased with it.' Sir William Ashburnham was delighted and talked of nothing but alterations in the deanery garden. Sir John Miller came round entirely. 'Damt,' he exploded to Richmond, 'I shall like a young dean.'[34]

The story of the deanery of Chichester, like the story of Lord Middlesex's canvass in the by-election for the county of

32. Austen to James Pelham, Salehurst, 24 Nov. 1741: 32698, fol. 376.
33. Ball to Newcastle, Chichester, 24 Nov. 1741: 32698, fols. 373–74.
34. Richmond to Newcastle, Goodwood, 25 Nov. 1741: 32698, fol. 377.

Sussex, ended merrily enough. It ended merrily enough, since this, being a true story, had to contain a few disappointments and afflictions. Ashburnham was Dean. Middlesex was facing the challenge of Thomas Sergison. Suddenly at Christmas, after advising with his friends, Sergison abruptly threw up the contest.[35] And without acquainting the old Duke of Somerset until the day after the decision was taken. The 'Monarch of Petworth'[36] was vastly provoked. He forwarded Sergison's note to his neighbor, Sir Cecil Bisshopp. He now altogether sank into the mire beneath the little grammar he knew. Bisshopp, he wrote, must be

> the better judge of the man and of his pretended reasons for deserting, if the undoubted rights and libertys of the subject and now perticularly of this countys freeholders against the most arbitrary and tyrannicall proceedings of those persons whoe have and thus doe trample upon and treat our freeholders, as if they were slaves (I hope noe Englishman will ever be) but take up a spiritt to withstand these petty shadow of things if Mr. Sergison had remembered his former declarations to all the freeholders from the highest to the lowest hee would not have soe very abruptly have given up soe righteous and glorious a caus as he hathe promise to endeavour to support but hee dosse now appear to be a gentleman not to bee depended upon by noe one freeholder in this county (except himselfe).

What sorrier things would yet appear to Sergison's disadvantage? 'These great men [Newcastle and his first friends] have agents whoe worketh like moals hidden under ground.' Detestable! And just at this auspicious moment, when Opposition to Sir Robert Walpole began to have 'a rising majority in the House of Commons', had wrested the chairmanship of the Committee of Elections and Privileges, and only four days

35. Sergison to Dorset, Lewes, 23 Dec. 1741: Sackville MSS.
36. Rev. Stephen Unwin to ———, 5 Aug. 1741: Sackville MSS.

ago had almost shattered Walpole's following by declaring the Westminster election 'voyd'. Astonished, to say the least, by the contents of Sergison's note, Somerset sent his servant to inform him that his letter deserved no answer. He ended his murky epistle by wishing Sir Cecil and all his family 'many and many Happy Christmasses'.[37]

Three weeks later Middlesex was returned unopposed for the county. To Lewes they came from the east and west, as Newcastle would have them, Henry Pelham, the Duke of Dorset, Jack Butler, Sir John Miller, Richmond, and many others, so that, as Newcastle said, the county might see 'who would have espoused our cause, if there had been occasion, and every body may know where the interest of the county is'. Newcastle did not of course mean to allude 'sillyly' to himself: his principles, his sense of belonging in Sussex to the right interest made him think first of what he called 'the solid, established, joint Whig interest, in the East and West'.[38] He himself could not come. The crisis over Sir Robert's continuance at the head of the ministry kept him in London. 'God knows,' he wrote darkly, 'how this will end. For my own part, I fear and dread the worst.'[39] Early in February Sir Robert resigned and retired to the Lords.

Mr. Barttelot, who had so yearned for the deanery, died, poor man, before Newcastle could make him a residentiary.[40] The Duke of Dorset bestowed his vicarage of Rottingdean upon young Thomas Curteis, and after long resentment against Newcastle for his inability to incline the King to the proposal, Dorset eventually procured for Thomas a stall at

37. Somerset to Bisshopp, Petworth, 26 Dec. 1741: Parham Papers, 57, Letters, 1708–1921. Addenda, Add. 178, 22–23; Addenda, Add. 194, 21. Thomas Stonestreet to William Ward, Lewes, 23 Dec. 1741: 32698, fol. 415.

38. Newcastle to Richmond, Claremont, 2 Jan. 1741/42: Goodwood MSS, Box 25.

39. Ibid., 9 Jan. 1741/42: Goodwood MSS, Box 25.

40. Daniel Walter to Newcastle, Cuckfield, 4 Nov. 1743: 32701, fol. 236.

Canterbury in 1755.[41] Thomas in 1747 succeeded his father at Sevenoaks. The Rev. Rice Williams was installed prebendary of Worcester in 1742, as the Archers wished. Canon Green, in spite of his small talk, received the extra £100 a year along with his coveted chaplaincy of the Royal Hospital at Chelsea in 1742,[42] and, the next year, was promoted to the prebend of Bury at Chichester, vacated by Maddox upon his translation from St. Asaph to Worcester.[43] Robert Austen, his senses alert, turned beggar for sure. He failed to get Westfield or Dallington or Rodmell or Icklesham or Nuthurst or Woodmancote. But in 1751 he did receive the living of Berwick and in 1778 Lord Pelham's Laughton. He died in 1786, fascinated by the history of Lewes, where apparently he held the rectory of St. Peter Westout.[44] Dean Ashburnham, as might be foreseen, became Bishop of Chichester. He had to await the publications of late nineteenth- and early twentieth-century church historians before his fame spread much farther than the diocese of Chichester. He held the see for a longer time than any other bishop of Chichester before or since. His persistent letters to Newcastle, in which he asked for additional preferment, established him as 'perhaps the most insistent of all clerical beggars'.[45] But the yearly value of both his deanery and bishopric was small, and Ashburnham had 'a large family growing up to want an education, which I am unable to afford'.[46] The very system may have made him importunate.

Members of the Sussex Opposition, defeated back in 1734,

41. Newcastle to Lord Halifax, 8 Aug. 1754: 32736, fol. 182 ff., Sykes, *Church and State,* pp. 175–76.

42. London County Council, *Survey of London, 11* (London, 1927), 55.

43. West Sussex County Record Office, 'Chapter Act Book', 4, 57.

44. William Lee, *History of Lewes* (Lewes, 1795), p. 358.

45. J. H. Overton and F. Relton, *The English Church . . . 1714–1800* (London, 1906), p. 159. Mary Bateson, 'Clerical Preferment under the Duke of Newcastle', *English Historical Review,* 7 (1892), 691.

46. Ashburnham to Newcastle, Chichester, 7 Oct. 1749: 32719, fol. 227.

also did well by the Duke. Newcastle's benignity and suasive influence may well have been immense. Sergison, for example, after an infinitude of moody overtures and negotiations, imagined that he preserved his independence by becoming Newcastle's man and accordingly sat for the borough of Lewes from 1747 until his death in 1766. John Fuller likewise succumbed to the Duke. He was a son of John Fuller who had trailed last for the county in the great election of 1734. In that year young Fuller had been old enough possibly to create trouble by supporting his father's cause. By the summer of 1740 he was quite definitely linked to his father as being in Opposition.[47] But in 1754, nine years after his father's death, John Fuller had changed sides, if side, indeed, there was left to change. He told Newcastle that he would not oppose him in the impending general election for the county of Sussex.[48] Delighted, the Duke nominated John Fuller to sit for his borough of Boroughbridge; and when, the next year, Fuller died, his friend and political associate, Sir Cecil Bisshopp, succeeded to Fuller's seat and represented Boroughbridge until 1768, the year of the Duke's death.

Thomas Ball never became either Chancellor or rector of Selsey. Greater honors awaited him. In 1746 there fell vacant the deanery of Worcester, a prize choicer by far than the deanery of Chichester. Accordingly, and with an eye to weakening the Tories in the Chapter of Worcester, at least twenty applicants, among them Henry Fox, the Lyttelton brothers, the Archbishop of Canterbury, the Duke of Marlborough, and Hardwicke himself, rushed headlong into the whirlpool of preferment-seekers to desire the King to give each of them the deanery for a dependent. Ball asked, and behind Ball his good friends Richmond and Maddox, now Bishop of Worcester, asked for him, too, and pressed Newcastle hard.[49] Another

47. R. Burnett to ——, Lewes, 18 July 1740: 32694, fol. 185.
48. Newcastle to the Earl of Northampton, Newcastle House, 15 March 1754: 32734, fol. 255; ibid., fol. 289.
49. Add. MSS 32708, fol. 158, and following letters.

round of the endless game had begun. But hold! The very thought of examining that round is exhausting. Mayhap, as Richmond feared, Newcastle and his brother were right: the deanery of Worcester, in spite of Ball's zeal, irreproachable life and character, his archdeaconry, and the former offer of the deanery of Chichester, might be 'too high a step for a country parson'.[50] Ball was passed over. He still hankered after the living of Selsey. Nothing, he assured Newcastle some weeks before Manningham's death vacated the living, should detach him from his obligations to his superiors or from his readiness to accept whatever they might judge most for the common cause. But perhaps Newcastle might

> be graciously pleased to renew your application in my favour to the Bishop for this favourite living upon a prospect of which (or of a snugg stall in any other near or midling church) I would most thankfully give up all pretentions to a higher station so graciously designed me here, being persuaded such a snugg adition to what I have already would enable me to do more for my great friends and be far better suited to the altered and un-happy state of my family . . . than I could hope for from the small accession of power or profit in the proposed elevation at Chichester.[51]

The Archdeacon appears to have known that at the right time both he and Ashburnham would be moved up. Ball's reward came in 1754.

Canon Parke and Henry Pelham died within a month of each other: Parke suddenly on December 20, 1753,[52] and Pelham after a courageous struggle, early in January. Thus death brought to Ball by right of seniority the vicarage of Amport, for which he resigned the living of Boxgrove in

50. Richmond to Newcastle, Goodwood, 19 Sept. 1746: 32708, fol. 338.
51. Ball to Newcastle, Chichester, 21 March 1749/50: 32720, fol. 147.
52. Dean Ashburnham to Newcastle, Albemarle Street, 25 Dec. 1753: 32733, fol. 563.

favor of that nephew of his, and he succeeded Parke as president of the Chapter. The death of Henry Pelham brought Newcastle to the Treasury. He now took command of the approaching general election. And, as before, his continued to be the task of rounding up the Sackville and Ashburnham interests in Sussex against the election there in May. Already, in concert with the new, young Duke of Richmond he had settled according to custom the future representation of Chichester, and the voters dutifully returned both a relative of the family at Goodwood and their own choice, John Page.[53] At long last the Duke had contrived the mysterious incorporation of Sussex politicians; his triumph by persuasion seemed complete. The county was a political microcosm of the nation. Actually, 'by 1754 there was no real opposition'.[54]

On March 20, 1754, Ball presided over a meeting of the canons residentiary in order to enact a solemn and profoundly useful bit of constitutional hocus-pocus. The see of Chichester was vacant by reason of Bishop Mawson's translation to Ely. Newcastle and the King had decided to put Ashburnham into the bishopric. Ball, permitted to keep his archdeaconry and his other trifles, was to be Dean. Such were the plans. But convention required that the plans become facts by means of constitutional rhetoric and ceremony. The Chapter had informed the King that Bishop Mawson had abdicated the diocese and that the throne of Chichester was thereby vacant. They had humbly supplicated His Majesty to grant them his fundamental leave and license to elect a new bishop and pastor. The Chapter duly received the King's letters under the great seal of Great Britain. On that day they decreed to proceed to the election and ordered their decree to be publicly affixed in the stall of every canon prebendary after the ancient manner. Then, the bell tolling according to accustomed usage,

53. Charles, third Duke of Richmond, to Newcastle, Hague, 7 May 1754: 32735, fol. 244.
54. Namier, *Structure of Politics* (2d ed.), p. 204.

President Ball and his brethren entered the Chapter House. Only eight prebendaries appeared. Ball pronounced the others contumacious and negligent and excluded them from having longer a voice in the election. The canons next heard the King's letters patent and letters missive, to wit:

> We of our princely disposition and zeal, being desirous to prefer unto the same see a person meet thereunto and considering virtue, learning, wisdom, gravity, and other good gifts wherewith our trusty and well beloved William Ashburnham . . . is endowed, we . . . recommend him unto you . . . We require you . . . to proceed to your election, according to the laws of this our realm, and our congé d'élire.

The President spoke: 'I, Thomas Ball . . . do give notice that all persons excommunicated, suspended, and interdicted, and others . . . who by right, custom or any like cause ought not to be present in this election, do depart from this Chapter House'. Ball pronounced the Chapter complete. The canons and prebendaries unanimously and with one consent nominated and then elected Ashburnham and gave power to William Wade publicly to declare to the clergy and people the aforesaid election.

President Ball and the canons then went out of the Chapter House, entered into the choir, and there listened both to a declaration and to the hymn *Te Deum*. Returning to the Chapter House, they decreed certain letters missive to be sent to the King, the Archbishop of Canterbury, and to William Ashburnham. Installation of the bishop followed a month later. Since Ball was shortly to become the new Dean,[55] Clarke had succeeded him in the presidency of the Chapter. At the west door of the cathedral Clarke met with the bishop-elect, a residentiary, nine prebendaries, two vicars choral, and other ministers of the church. They listened to letters commissional

55. West Sussex County Record Office, 'Chapter Act Book', *4*, 170.

100

from the Archbishop of Canterbury: His Grace therein confirmed according to the custom of the church. Ashburnham took a corporal oath upon the holy Evangelists of fidelity and allegiance 'to our sovereign George the Second . . . and of renouncing, refusing, and abjuring all . . . manner of foreign jurisdiction, power, authority, and superiority according to the . . . Act of Parliament', and swore to defend the Church. Now satisfied, the clergy proceeded up the nave to the choir. Clarke enthroned Mr. Ashburnham in the episcopal seat. Whereupon the clergy took the oath of canonical obedience to the Lord Bishop of Chichester.[56] Dean Ball was not mentioned among those present.

What with the vicarage of Eartham, his archdeaconry, the deanery, and 'the great living of Amport' Ball was now comfortably off. His duties as one of Newcastle's agents were no longer necessary. His two daughters married well. He grew old, retaining, in spite of his demented wife, his conviviality. At the very last, in 1770, he settled down to devise his properties in and near Chichester; he arranged bequests to his family, his friends, and his servant; he considered the disposal of his plate, chinaware, liquor, his manuscripts and books, and the portrait of his special friend and patron, Isaac Maddox.[57] Then just before he died he revealed a flash of his old genius. He resigned the deanery in favor of his son-in-law. George III and the Chapter enacted his wish.[58]

56. West Sussex County Record Office, 'Chapter Act Book', *4*, 158–68.
57. P.C.C., Jenner, 442.
58. Hayley, *Memoirs, 1*, 106–08. West Sussex County Record Office, 'Chapter Act Book', *4*, 300. P.R.O., S.P. 44/154, fol. 286.

EPILOGUE

THUS, while the guns of the Royal Navy rumbled the oceans and the Continent shook with universal war, tremors, beginning at the Star in Lewes and in Chichester Close upon the news of the deaths of Butler and Hargraves, crisscrossed Sussex and, becoming a small earthquake, reached to Knole in Kent, jarred Newcastle's pagoda of patronage up in London, and thrust onwards to distant Worcester, there to stir dust on the stalls of the cathedral. Through connection of one man with another the late anxious affair of the deanery and the by-election came almost to embrace the whole nation. It brought into the open the so nicely distinguished gradations within the structure of subordination. It showed how intimately a man's fortunes, even his principles, were affected by his friends, patrons, and batches of relatives. The case of the deanery no less than the by-election for the county made clear that Newcastle and his friends had to work for their victories. The expectation of meeting difficulty, not the 'degenerate fondness for tricking short-cuts', made eighteenth-century politicians liberal men.

For the homunculi of Sussex were not all intimidated, nor were they all bought, least of all the freeholders. If they were seldom disinterested in their politics, it was not so much that they could not afford the luxury of disinterestedness as that they had almost no politics to be disinterested about. In 1741 they had no newspaper, published in Sussex, to translate national issues into local terms. They were utterly remote in point both of time and receptivity from that day when Mr. Cobden would be talking about Corn Laws in the metropolitan press or Mr. Gladstone about the horrid Bimbashis and Kaimakans. There was virtually nothing to cry up or to cry down except the great county families or now and then the exposure of a Jacobite. And in Sussex, unlike Northampton-shire,[1] their leaders, impatient at the senescent dubieties of Somerset at Petworth, were looking in increasing numbers to the head of the house of Pelham. Newcastle's very mastery of their local Church and State rested on the knowledge, which he rarely forgot, that ultimately the voters were free men: they had something to sell—votes—and the votes must be acquired. They sold those votes on occasion for cash. More generally, they bartered them for purposes of protection or investment: a house over one's head, the continuing tenure of one's fields or pastures, the prospects that a ship might be built in the borough, another customer found among the neighboring gentry, drink and entertainment at the big house, and the pleasure of being applied to in person by the candi-dates and the agents of the dukes. At election time, as Ball noticed, every freeholder looked upon himself as 'a sort of gentleman . . . and a man of very great consequence'.[2]

Whence the contract of honor: the contract made habitually in the eighteenth century between one gentleman and another, sometimes at the expense of a third: 'service is obligation, obligation implies return'.[3] The contract of honor explained why the humblest voters intended to keep their promises; it bound men for the time being into a political party; and it was expected to govern the relations between the King and his ministers. What a man was socially depended on his status, although in England God, if He chose, might call him to a better one. In the lower reaches of the structure of subordina-tion the contract of honor described political relations only. Because he owed his preferment to the Duke of Newcastle,

1. Eric G. Forrester, *Northamptonshire County Elections and Elec-tioneering, 1695–1832* (London, Oxford University Press, 1941), p. 7.

2. Ball to Isaac Maddox, 3 Oct. 1733: 32688, fols. 447–48. Robson, *Oxfordshire Election of 1754*, p. 22.

3. John Carswell and Lewis Arnold Dralle, eds., *The Political Diary of George Bubb Dodington* (Oxford, Clarendon Press, 1965), 21 June 1754, p. 281.

the new vicar of Ringmer offered to one of the Duke's agents the nomination of a curate to assist him;[4] Hargraves sought to do Canon Backshell's uncle a favor because Backshell had found a living for Hargraves' curate;[5] because John Cheesman and his family had supported Newcastle's interest 'time immemorial', he asked him to approach the Commissioners of the Excise so that he might be employed for the season in collecting the hop duty;[6] if Newcastle would arrange matters so that poor Mr. Stuart might hold two livings without having to pay the costs of a dispensation, he promised his 'inviolable attachments' to the Duke 'not only upon this but upon any future occasion'.[7] Both Newcastle and Bishop Mawson believed that one good turn deserved another. To respect a contract was to stick to one's principles. 'My honour,' Sergison insisted when negotiating his treaty with Newcastle, 'is as dear and sacred to me as his is.'[8] Society, as Burke said, was indeed a contract. Preferments were often so many political debts paid up in accordance with a gentleman's agreement.

The memory of the clergy in eighteenth-century Sussex was not only chiseled into tablets of the diocesan churches. It was preserved in Additional Manuscripts 32686 ff. Therein are at once their principal memorial and their shame; the begging Barttelots and Ashburnhams, preserved in Pelham's name (pretty! in amber to observe dirt, grubs, or worms). Granted that Ball by any standard was abject, although accomplished. But the clerical players of musical chairs, not being extraordinary men, moved in accordance with the rules long ago set for them. The higher clergy (they were not all rich) played for the sport and in the persuasion that they were being statesmen. The lesser clergy—: 'in Sussex,' Ball wrote,

---

4. Hargraves to Newcastle, 8 Nov. 1733: 32689, fol. 11.
5. Hargraves to ———, Chichester, 7 March 1740/1: 32696, fols. 200–01.
6. Cheesman to Newcastle, 11 July 1740: 32693, fol. 479.
7. Ball to Newcastle, Chichester, 21 Sept. 1740: 32695, fols. 113–14.
8. Sergison to William Poole, Cuckfield, 25 Nov. 1746: 32709, fol. 267.

'where we have so many small livings'; 'starvings' were most of the benefices at Chichester.[9] Large families, impoverishment, too few professions to enter, a slack, sometimes failing economy, the hardened habit of deference, the gratifications of electioneering, a parochial outlook, complacency of spirit, and always in that small population the personal relationship, not the cash nexus, as the knot of society—these circumstances, taken together, far more than greed or corruption, explain why the clergy surrendered willingly to the Duke of Newcastle. To that affable conquest the canons and dignitaries of Chichester Cathedral contributed significantly. Certainly they never imagined that each man should count for one and for no more than one. So careful of precedent in their transactions, they were perhaps careless, to say the least, in picking the best man for a benefice. It sufficed that his principles were sound and his character unexceptionable. The canons and dignitaries disposed of ecclesiastical offices, even as laymen disposed of both ecclesiastical and civil, according to their sense of personal obligation. They went about, as Tillotson had advised, doing good. How could they help it if first of all they did good to themselves and their friends? Ultimately and beyond the spiteful little hatreds, the administration of Sussex was held together by friendship, sometimes by love.

Canon Clarke was no lickspittle. In 1767, at the age of seventy, he dedicated his learned book, *The Connexion of the Roman, Saxon, and English Coins,* to Newcastle. The language of his dedication might seem to have been a courtier's rhetoric. It was merely the polite way of addressing a great duke in public. The sentiments were genuine and sprang from more than forty years of knowledge of his patron. 'The honour you do me,' Clarke wrote,

> in permitting me to address these papers to you, I look upon as a real addition to the obligations I have received.

9. W. D. Peckham, 'The Parishes of the City of Chichester', *S.A.C.,* 74 (1933), 65–97.

It gives me a public opportunity of saying, that I am truly thankful for them; and that they were not the effects of importunity, but owing to that disposition of doing good to others, that spirit of beneficence, by which your Grace is so remarkably distinguished . . . Your generous and affable deportment in private life,—your temperate use of power, in the many high stations you have so deservedly filled . . . your universal application and integrity in the discharge of these offices,—your candour and benevolence towards your enemies,—your zeal for the service of your friends,—and above all, for the religion and liberties of your country, are such examples as must be received with universal approbation.

Newcastle replied in a private letter: '*Laudari à laudato viro maxima laus est.* It has been my misfortune, not to have had it in my power, for my own sake, as well as for that of the publick, to bring you into a more exalted station in your profession. I have had the greatest regard and friendship for you; you have now laid me under an obligation which I can never forget.'[10]

10. Newcastle to Clarke, Claremont, 6 April 1767: Nichols, *Literary Anecdotes, 4, 379.*

APPENDIX

The Reverend Thomas Ball to the Duke of Richmond

My Lord Duke,   Chichester, 13 October 1741

Your Grace's most obliging message came too late and was of too much moment to admit of a full answer by the last post and as there does not appear any immediate danger of death in my friend the Dean I hope your Grace will the more easily excuse this short delay in my acknowledgements for it. I am infinitely obliged to your Grace and my other great friends for the high honour and favour first designed me in case of a vacancy here and in return beg leave to assure you all that I would not decline any station in which I could be further serviceable to your interest, however unworthy I might think myself of it in other respects and however inconsiderable it might appear to me in point of personal advantage. But I can't see, my Lord Duke, how it could possibly answer your ends or my own unless I could keep my archdeaconry and some other little things I now enjoy along with the deanery, which either the law or at least my superiours might perhaps disallow of. As Archdeacon and Judge of the Ecclesiastical Court I have a pretty considerable intercourse with and influence over members of the clergy, churchwardens, and other freeholders in this half of the county, whereas the authority and interest of a Dean of Chichester, as such, is infinitely less extensive and chiefly confined to this city and suburbs and even there I cannot conceive he has any greater capacity of doing good offices or engaging more persons to his interest than an active and hospitable residentiary with the same spirit and fortune. The Dean has but just the same share with a residentiary in the disposal of all the offices, places, and per-ferments belonging to the Church and I have often observed that one is apter to make enemies than friends by having the power of punishing delinquents and exercising even the necessary points of Quire discipline over the respective inferiour officers. This I apprehend is a true state of the case with respect to my present and future proposed capacity of serving my friends on the supposition of my not holding both and I shall only add with respect to myself that the exchange would not in all probability advance my income above ten pounds a year certain for which I must be 250 or 300 £ out of pocket presently, leave, what I think, a more convenient house to my brother *Parke,* after haveing just expended above 400 £ upon it and be obliged to live in a less eligible because in a more envyed and shewy situation. If indeed I were allowed to keep everything I now have except my Residentiaryship along with the Deanery it might doubtless give an additional influence in favour of my great friends and the common cause and I might be made whole agen in about two years time; but this I only mention to shew your Grace (and if you please any other great friends through your hands) how the case would really stand on the most advantageous supposition, having no particular inclination at all to the Deanery on any terms, much less on such as might appear engrossing or unprecedented, so that if, as I don't in the least doubt, my superiours can as effectually answer their own and the publick purposes any other way and oblige us with an able and good Whig Governour it will be full as agreeable to me; I shall ever retain a gratefull sense of the honour as well as the high trust and confidence reposed in me by this intended overture not doubting the future assistence of such good friends in any other reasonable addition I might hereafter desire to the great happiness I already enjoy through their good offices and intercession.

I have now, my Lord, fully and frankly laid before your Grace the exact state of the case and my own unfeigned sentiments on an event that will I doubt happen ere long; I will only beg leave to add that notwithstanding all this, I entirely submit myself to the superiour judgment and direction of your Grace and my other great friends in this and every other affair of this sort, not being actuated by selfish views and to save expence but with a general view to your interest in what I have alledged, being always determined to accept of any station on the most disadvantageous terms to myself if you should expect it of me, as most for your own and the publick service.

If (as I secretly wish on your accounts as well as our own) another of our body, who is at present unprovided with a house, should be pitched upon to succeed poor Dean Hargraves, I should be glad for your Grace's sake especially, to be apprized of it as soon as possible because I have good reason to fear a certain candidate will be set up for the vacant Residentiaryship and the Duke of Newcastle much pestered for him by Mr. Hutchins Williams and perhaps some others, and Mr. Parke if not my brother Backshell are well disposed to him already, though should he succeed there would soon be an entire end of the Whigg chapter and the publick interest as far as he could effect either, and he would as a creature of Williams, at least and out of principle too do all possible prejudice to the general interest and your Grace's especially at Chichester.

This consideration was my only inducement to give you this early and otherwise impertinent hint in an affair so much out of my sphere and on a supposition of Mr. Clarke's remove which I have no sort of authority for. I have no particular and proper prebendary to propose but hope for your own sakes as well as ours care will be taken to preserve an indisputable majority of true Whiggs in the Chapter of Chichester.

I am, my Lord Duke, with the utmost esteem and gratitude
Your Grace's most obedient and obliged humble servant

Tho. Ball

INDEX

Main references to persons appear in italic type.

Abergavenny, William Nevill, 16th Baron of, 54

Adams, Rev. George, Prebendary of Chichester, 74–75, 79–80

Amport, Hampshire, vicarage of, 11, 28, 98, 101

Archer, Henry, 90, 96

Archer, Thomas, M. P. for Bramber, 34, 89–90, 96

Ashburnham, family of, 3, 83

Ashburnham, John Ashburnham, 2nd Earl of, 81

Ashburnham, Rev. William, Dean of Chichester, 80–82, 84–86, 92, 104; appointed Dean, 93, 94; raised to bishopric of Chichester, 96, 98–101

Ashburnham, Sir William, Bt., 3, 81, 93

Austen, Rev. Robert, 91–93, 96

Backshell, Rev. John, 16–17, 18–22, 23, 24, 25, 29, 68, 72, 74, 75, 104

Ball, Lawrence, 61

Ball, Rev. Thomas, Archdeacon and Canon Residentiary of Chichester, later Dean of, 13, 16, 17, 18–22, 23–24, 25, 26, 29, 32, 59–88, 89, 91, 93, 103, 104–05; admitted to prebend of Hampstead, 14; becomes Dean, 99–101; President of the Chapter, 99–100; seeks deanery of Worcester, 97–98

Barttelot, family of, 3, 8, 53

Barttelot, Rev. Walter, 41, 75, 95; asks to succeed Hargraves in the Deanery, 6, 59, 89, 104; his political

interest, 8–9; seeks canon residentiaryship of Chichester, 7

Bisshopp, Sir Cecil, Bt., 3, 5, 26, 42–44, 45, 50, 65, 88, 94–95, 97

Board, John, 54, 55, 84

Bowers, Rev. Thomas, Bishop of Chichester, 12, 39, 86, 88

Bowyer, William, 77

Brockbank, Rev. Thomas, 92

Brudenell, James, M. P. for Chichester, 66–67

Butler, James, M. P. for Sussex, 21, 34, 42–46, 48, 50, 66, 67, 69, 71, 102

Butler, John, 46, 54, 95

Cheesman, John, 104

Chenevix, Mrs. Mary, 68

Chichester, City of, 3; St. Mary's Hospital, 14, 19–20, 19 n. 45, 21, 25, 64

Chichester, Dean and Chapter of, 14–15, 17, 18, 19, 21–22, 23, 24, 25, 28, 29, 79, 93, 99–101; constitution of, 10; electoral influence, 11–13, 16, 56, 73; estates, 11

Chichester, Diocese of: Bishops, *see under* Bowers, Thomas; Waddington, Edward; Hare, Francis; Mawson, Matthias; Deans, *see under* Sherlock, Thomas; Newey, John; Hayley, Thomas; Hargraves, James; Ashburnham, William; Ball, Thomas; Harward, Charles

Clarke, Rev. William, Canon Residentiary and later Chancellor of Chichester, 19, 25, 29, 60, 72, 74–75,